THE SCIENCE OF
PSYCHOLOGY

k
kandour

This edition published by
Kandour Ltd
1-3 Colebrooke Place
London N1 8HZ
United Kingdom

2004 Kandour Ltd

Created by Metro Media Ltd
5 Upper Wimpole Street
London W1G 6BP
info@metromediauk.com

Managing editors: Emma Hayley, Jenny Ross
Author: Emma Steiger
Editorial assistance: Sarah Kane
Illustrations: Emmett Elvin

Cover design: George Georgiou
Content design: Jenny Ross and George Georgiou
Page layout: Jenny Ross

Doodle contributions: Andrew Adamides, Dawn Barnett, Dan Brinzac at Rex Features (Clooney doodle),
Robert Collins, Tony Coombes, Mark Donnelly, Adam Fraser, Emma Hayley, Laura Henderson, Chad Mount,
Brenda Ponnay, Brenda Ross, Sue Ross, Samantha Wallis, Susannah Wise.

With thanks to:
Paul Tranter and Victoria Grimsell

Our thanks to Epilepsy Action and The Neurofibromatosis Association
who have given permission for use of the celebrity doodles. These doodles were created in
support of National Doodle Day 2004 helping to raise funds for the two charities.
For details go to **www.nationaldoodleday.org.uk**

© Kandour Ltd

Printed and bound in United Kingdom

ISBN 1-904756-20-4

THE SCIENCE & PSYCHOLOGY OF

CONTENTS

Celebrity doodles

p 23: Sir Richard Branson, Greg Wise. p28: Dick Francis. p29: Ralph Steadman, Louis de Bernieres, Glenda Jackson. p39: Wayne Bridge, Tom Conti. p40: Maeve Binchy, Brenda Blethyn. p45: Gillian Anderson. p53: Julie Walters, George Clooney. p57: Desmond Morris. p59: Uri Geller. p62: Helena Bonham-Carter, Charles Dance. p75: Jilly Cooper, Lynn Redgrave. p77: Frank Lampard, Carol Smilie. p79: Steve Davis, Sir Roger Moore. p87: Patti Boulaye. p95: Jeffrey Archer, Jeremy Irons. p101: Betty Driver, Clare Short. p102: Elton John, Brian Blessed, Ron Moody. p103: Alan Bennett, Phil Collins, Richard E Grant, Twiggy. p108: Joanna Lumley. p118: Manolo Blahnik. p123: The Duchess of York. p124: Claudia Schiffer. p126: Jonathan Ross. p132: Ken Bruce. p133: Edward Fox.

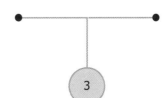

THE SCIENCE & PSYCHOLOGY OF

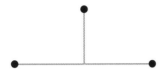

FOREWORD

Your doodles really can tell you something about your personality. While, in some cases, you may not like or believe what they mean, they are a way that your unconscious communicates with you.

All sorts of people doodle and in lots of different circumstances. In this book you will find doodles from around the world, and from a host of celebrities. The doodles of artists, actors, musicians, playwrights, authors, politicians, designers and royalty are featured.

In the following pages read about why the page positioning and size of your doodles are relevant, how pen pressure can help to determine your personality type and which eminent analysts used doodle interpretation as part of their therapies.

Just as dreams contain coded symbols that psychoanalysts interpret, doodles have their own meanings. In this A–Z you'll find hundreds of different types of doodles from houses to horses and snakes to snowmen. Each entry suggests a meaning, an emotion, a message, a desire, a fantasy, or a character trait that you may possess. Most importantly it uncovers coded messages from your unconscious, which can help you to understand yourself better.

So grab yourself a pen and a notepad, or a newspaper, or a napkin or even some kitchen roll, and get doodling.

Doodle on...

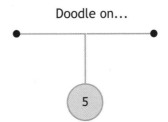

THE SCIENCE & PSYCHOLOGY OF

What is a doodle?

And what do your doodles say about you?

When Freud invented the technique of psycho-analysis, he interpreted to the patient the meaning of what the patient said to him. When psychoanalysis was extended to the treatment of children, the therapist interpreted the meaning of children's play. Doodles are a kind of play in a visual form. Like slips of the tongue, dreams, the forgetting of names and neurotic symptoms, they are spontaneous desires that Freud believed came from childhood, which need to find expression and realise themselves in a disguised form.

Jung also regarded dreams as communications from the unconscious. But to the individual unconscious of Freud, he added the concept of the 'collective unconscious', which has evolved over time to contain the inherited wisdom of race. This takes the form of visual

"For it is the function of consciousness not only to recognise and assimilate the external world through the gateway of the senses, but to translate into visible reality the world within us." Jung

eruptions of thought and feeling that we do not know we have.

This raises the question of the 'I' in relation to agency. Freud argued that the conscious ego was not master in its own house, but acted as the unknowing instrument of repressed unconscious wishes. He compared its situation to a rider on a runaway horse.

It was a theory that Freud developed in his famous interpretation of dreams. The 'manifest content' is the dream as we remember and report it. But behind this lies the 'latent content', consisting of the repressed sexual

images or 'archetypes', as he called them, which are not of our making but impress themselves upon us, often through dreams. He therefore took a much more positive attitude to the dream than Freud who interpreted it as a neurotic symptom. Instead, Jung viewed dreams as a way the unconscious tells the conscious that a part of the personality is being neglected or unrealised. Jung was a believer that the path to true self or personality — he did not believe that personality was a given but instead something we all have to strive for — was manifested by 'definiteness,

THE SCIENCE & PSYCHOLOGY OF

wholeness and ripeness'.

This wholeness is attained when all parts of the psyche are in balance. He introduced the terms 'introvert' and 'extravert' into psychology as defining psychological types, and later suggested that the psyche operated through four functions: thinking, feeling, sensation and intuition. Any one of these functions can be predominant in an individual's way of dealing with an experience. For example, you might be an 'extraverted intuitive', an 'introverted thinker', or an 'introverted feeling' type. There are eight possible mutations which Jung identified.

"My doodling is definitely about trying to create some kind of unconscious order... trying to make complicated patterns symmetrical...like a nervous ordering tic while I'm thinking and talking..." Novelist

Jung believed that habitual attitudes were nearly always taken too far. This means that the thinker would neglect his feelings while the intuitive paid too little attention to the facts given by sensation. Someone who over-valued thinking might alienate himself from his emotional roots. Introverts were caught up in their inner worlds, while extraverts lost themselves in external events.

When the unconscious decides to give the conscious a warning, be it in the form of dreams, neurotic symptoms and the like, Jung believed that they are expressions of the 'other side' trying to assert itself. There is, therefore, within everyone, a desire to strive

for unity. Divisions should be replaced by consistency, opposites equally balanced, the conscious in equilibrium with the unconscious. This, he believed, was the basis of personality. Only once you have achieved this wholeness and unity within yourself can you actually achieve 'personality'.

It is with this backdrop in mind that one might seek to know oneself a little better. Doodle interpretation may not be the most common of ways to understand who we are, but the nature of doodles are such that they are a valid medium to do so. While it has been commonly thought that dreams reveal the workings of the unconscious mind, doodles have been less valued as performing the very same function. However, highly regarded analysts have used doodling as part of their therapeutic methods.

Jung developed a technique called 'active imagination', encouraging his patients to enter a state of euphoria, in which they would still be conscious but their judgment suspended. They were then asked by Jung to draw and paint their fantasies. The technique helped his patients to rediscover hidden parts of themselves. Their unconscious, therefore, was breaking through and translating itself visually onto paper. Jung was the first analyst to supplement verbal analysis with this method. Others followed and the increasing use of painting, modelling and music in therapy is testimony to the success of Jung's methods.

While doodles are generally penned in absent-mindedness rather than in a state of euphoria, they are similar in that they are spontaneous forms of expression. It is this

INTRODUCTION

spontaneity that lends itself to analysis. The eminent psychoanalyst, Donald Winnicott, used doodles as a way of analysing his child patients, which became known as 'the squiggle' technique. He would start by making a mark on paper, then the child was encouraged to continue the doodle he had started. Afterwards he would interpret its meaning. Winnicott was highly respected in his field and The Squiggle Foundation survives him.

Before Winnicott, the Rorschach test was devised by the Swiss psychiatrist, Hermann Rorschach, as a way of diagnosing psychological types. He drew up ten symmetrical ink blots. From the way his patients saw these standard images Rorschach interpreted the structure of their minds. The list is still used in many European countries.

Another method, graphology, has been used for centuries to evaluate personality types. If the slant or heaviness of your handwriting can tell a graphologist information about who you are, then so too can doodles.

When we talk about a doodle, most of us visualise the scrawls we do when we're concentrating, or when we're bored. More often than not we will scribble when we're on the phone, in a meeting or listening intently in a lecture hall. Such doodles are usually consigned to the wastepaper basket eventually, however they are of significance as they can provide a gateway into our unconscious, revealing personality traits and hidden emotions, desires and fantasies.

Doodles should not be confused with artist's sketches or finished works of art (no matter how much they might look like a doodle). The main distinction is that a doodle

"If I have to sit still and listen without doodling, I usually don't hear a word and certainly don't retain anything that is being said. Not doodling causes an anxious feeling that overpowers my ability to concentrate."
Artist

is done spontaneously, without even thinking. A sketch, however, may be a first stage in the creation of a piece of art and therefore contrived. A finished work of art is thought about often for hours on end and might be re-worked a number of times. For instance, when the Spanish painter, Pablo Picasso scribbled on a napkin to pay for a restaurant bill, it was done in an instant with little thought behind it. It was spontaneous and therefore can be classified as a doodle.

It seems that we know much more than we think we know. But the 'language' of the unconscious is coded and often visual rather than verbal. Some of the archetypes are universal symbols, recurrent in mythology. But the unconscious may also fasten on small, insignificant things, like doodles. This A–Z of doodles, while making no claim to be either definitive or authoritative, provides a kind of mesh, a suggestive mesh, through which perhaps you can see, not the doodle, but the thing-in-itself that lies behind it. This book is an attempt to introduce you to yourself. For as Lévi-Strauss observed of myth: "When the mind is left to commune with itself and no longer has to come to terms with objects, it is in a sense reduced to imitating itself as object."

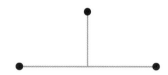

How do you doodle?

While what you doodle is significant, so too is where you doodle in relation to the page. Your doodles are likely to be scrawled on a number of different mediums, and under different circumstances — on the agenda for a meeting, on a napkin, on a newspaper, in the margins of books or manuscripts and so on.

Through history people doodled in all sorts of places. The monks doodled in the margins of ancient manuscripts, Leonardo Da Vinci doodled around the sketches of his inventions, original drafts of famous novels show the authors' doodles surrounding the text.

While these doodles are being penned absent-mindedly perhaps either in concentration, or boredom, or nervousness, the author of the doodle is not only creating pretty patterns, but a series of coded messages that if deciphered tell their own story. The placement of the doodle on the page and the pressure of the pen are as relevant as the symbols in the doodle, and reveal certain elements of personality. If your doodle is in the centre of the page, it suggests you are an extravert, perhaps attention-seeking, suiting

"I have very dark, sad, angry drawings and silly, happy drawings. I think my doodles express my emotions better than I do."
Actress

"I doodle during long meetings, I doodle in coffee shops, I doodle on vacation to remember the places I've been..."
Illustrator

a profession that requires speaking in public — an actress, barrister or in public relations for example. Beginning in a central spot on the page may also be an expression of a need for some space. You want to withdraw from restrictive, suffocating situations and need to have an outlet for your ever-increasing creative ideas. If your doodles are placed at the top of the page, it reveals you are confident, dynamic, and full of ideas. If the doodle has been penned next to a title or heading, it can show that you think you have something more important to say than the subject of the paper. Perhaps you feel superior to the person who has written the paper. The left hand side of the page, or in the margins is a common place to find doodles. It could be evidence of some nostalgia for the past. Doodling on the right hand side of the page is less common. It can show that you have a strong urge to express yourself, or communicate your innermost thoughts. Doodling at the bottom of the page indicates introversion and a lack of confidence.

The pressure of the pen is also significant in analysing doodles. Very heavy pressure

INTRODUCTION

would indicate that you are interested in concrete reality, in things that you can see, hear, feel and taste i.e. that are material. You are likely to be an outdoorsy type and interested in sporting pursuits. You are suited to being in a profession where you can gauge material results and achievements. Everyone else comes second to this in your life. There is a primitive element present in your personality. You are likely to have a hearty appetite and react to everything that appeals to your senses — you are animalistic in your urges. Your materialism extends to people, who you see as possessions. You are generally a pioneer in your field, leading the pack. You are a doer, rather than a thinker.

A medium-heavy pressure suggests that your interest is divided between people and material things. A light pressure tells us that you are a deeply sensitive soul. Your approach

to life is far more cautious than that of the doodler using a heavy pen pressure. Your interest is primarily in people. You exhibit introversion, and you are a thinker rather than a doer. If the pressure of your doodles is erratic, it could point to emotional instability.

The size of your doodles is also relevant. Large doodles show extraversion — your energies flow outward and you are more active rather than pensive. You get a handle on a new person, situation or plan in its

entirety, without getting caught up in the detail. It also exhibits extravagance — either with yourself or you may lavish gifts on others. Small doodles show that you scrutinise everything in minute detail. You tend to be introverted and would suit a profession with minimum contact with other people. You probably prefer to live alone and find it more difficult to achieve intimacy with someone. Your introversion means that most of your energy is put into thinking rather than doing.

Now discover what the symbols in your doodles mean in the 'Analysing your doodles' A–Z that follows on page 13.

DOODLE DICTIONARY

ANALYSING YOUR DOODLES A–Z

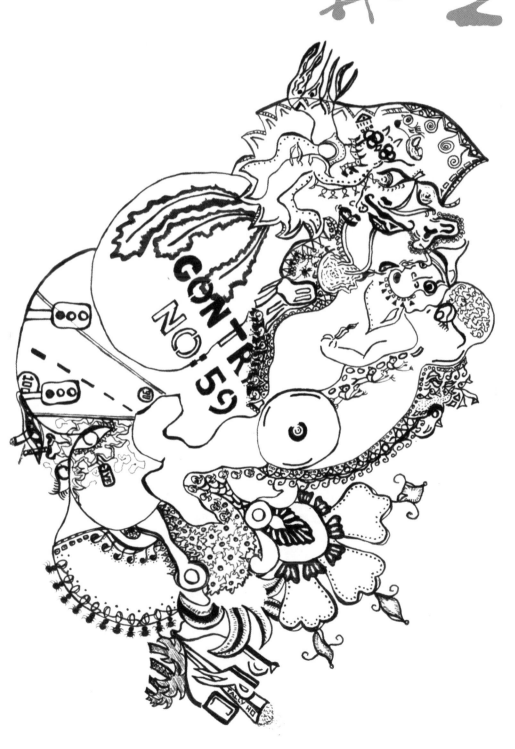

Abstracts and patterns

These types of intricate, abstract doodles can take various forms. The first shows individual lines, symbols and patterns connected together to form one cohesive, self-contained pattern. Such intricate doodles may signal a desire to resolve a conflict in your life. By connecting the different parts of the doodle together, you unconsciously attempt to tie up loose ends in your own life.

You may also try to make patterns symmetrical, which represents a desire to bring order to your life. The use of black and white blocks to form symmetrical patterns such as black and white squares (chessboards), within these abstract doodles represents the polarity of the human psyche, and of pairs of opposites such as:

chaos and order, good and evil, odd and even. These doodles represent your attempt to put together irreconcilable opposites and unify divisions in your relationships. Once you have completed this type of doodle, you often feel an enormous sense of satisfaction. It's almost as if a complex mathematical equation has been solved – representing the conflict in your life. Even if nothing actually has been resolved in reality during the process of doodling, you nonetheless feel that something has changed. These kinds of doodles, therefore, often have a therapeutic effect.

What else does this say specifically about your personality? You are probably in a creative profession, and highly imaginative. You are likely to be determined, ambitious and know what you want from life. You also tend to be fairly controlling.

ANALYSING YOUR DOODLES

With the second type of self-contained doodle (left, bottom), where you link shapes and patterns to create symmetry, you don't stop until the entire page is filled. This reflects the same personality traits as the first doodle i.e. a desire to resolve conflict, ambitious, determined and fairly controlling, but also a tendency towards the obsessive. Within the pattern you may see individual swirls, dots, circles, zigzag lines, straight lines, stars and so on. While each has their own meaning, the predominant feature of the pattern as a whole is its symmetry and repetition. The third type of abstract doodle (shown on this page) takes elements of the self-contained, cohesive doodle, but the doodle lacks the rigid lines and symmetry. If the doodle seems less 'finished', it may represent a desire to tolerate conflicts and demonstrate that you are not keen on controlling

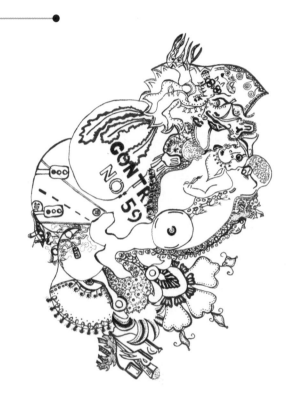

circumstances in your life or other people. You have a tendency to let people behave as they want and have the capacity to accept others' faults and weaknesses, sometimes to your own detriment. Lots of white space symbolises a lack of vision and uncertainty of the future. If the pattern is particularly swirly, it shows you possess a lot of creative energy but have less of a definite idea of what to do with it. You tend not to be good at planning and have more of a sense of freedom.

Note: The symbols in each of these abstract doodles can be analysed separately. For example you'll see chessboards, swirls, lines, stars, dots, a tomato, a butterfly, an octopus, a musical symbol, a flower etc. all of which have their own meanings.

Aeroplane

This is a symbol of change. It represents a need to escape and 'spread your wings' elsewhere. It is usually doodled by someone who thinks 'the grass is always greener on the other side'. It shows a desire to flee from a present situation and way of life.

You may feel disillusioned with your present life and the limitations it has brought with it. A plane represents a desire to leave the past in the past, to escape events, and to move forward to a new life. It would usually be penned by someone who is willing to take risks, and is independent. A plane in motion or pointing upwards indicates an optimist, full of energy and willing to take on new possibilities in life. The new journey you wish to embark on

may be a new relationship, or a search for somewhere new to live. Whichever it represents, your plans may not necessarily come to fruition, and this may already be anticipated by you. Thus a plane falling from the sky or shown crashing would show you are anxious about change. This type of plane would reveal your pessimistic character, resigned to a future of failure. It can also represent a lack of self-confidence, or of shattered dreams and hopes. A war or attacking plane, may mean you are feeling criticised by others, and/or you are feeling angry and frustrated. The aeroplane is generally doodled by men, and is a phallic symbol. It usually means that you have a high sex drive, but that your desires are not being satisfied. This type of doodle, therefore, may represent sexual frustration.

Alien

An alien can represent forces that are beyond control; a fear of the unknown or the anticipation of an important meeting. That meeting may be with the 'self' and is concerned with finding the greater potential in yourself. Aliens are either thought of as scary beings or as a representation of an exciting 'other' world. Depending on how you view aliens, the doodle either means you are feeling emotions that are difficult to identify with, you may be feeling scared about a change in your life — and not sure of its outcome. Alternatively, you wish to go on an exciting new adventure.

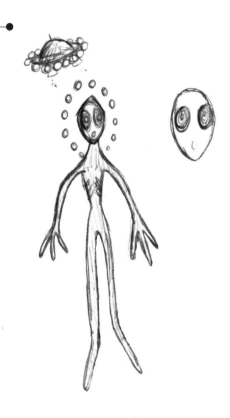

Angel

Angels are said to be God's messengers. They can be symbols of good luck, and may indicate that a birth is about to happen. They can also represent your feelings about death, heaven and the after-life.

The expression 'guardian angel' is significant, as drawing an angel can be an expression of a desire to be guided by a parental figure if you are on the brink of making an important decision.

Angels are usually doodled by females, who are romantics and dreamy. Angels have obvious associations with peace, purity and innocence, as well as religious connotations.

Animals

What kind of animal do you doodle? Is it cute and cuddly, or ugly and aggressive? Cute, cuddly animals shows your caring side. You are sensitive to the needs of others, and like to defend your friends. You are probably an animal lover.

Wild, angry-looking animals represent sexual urges, fear, anger and survival. A hurt or wounded animal usually mirrors your feelings. You may be so wounded emotionally, that you feel you want to withdraw.

Alligator

The alligator or crocodile represents a feeling of being attacked or overburdened. It is often the case that you have an overbearing mother or father. It can also represent deceit.

Ant

Ants are extremely organised, efficient and hard-working just like you, or at least this is how you would like to be seen by others. However, the ant may show that you are feeling insignificant, or small — you feel like an ant among a throng of other ants. It may just be you're being plagued by small annoyances and worries. More profoundly, the ant can reveal a deep self-loathing. You may fear sex or feel it is dirty.

Ape

An ape can represent deceit. Your unconscious may be trying to tell you that you or someone close to you is being deceitful. You may have the feeling that you are being taken advantage of in some way. Take it as a warning sign.

An ape, if drawn as a wild, aggressive animal, can represent the selfish urges in you such as greediness. You may be prone to mischievousness.

The ape can also reveal great intuition and wisdom about relationships and friendships.

Apple

The apple is the fruit that tempted Adam and Eve in the garden of Eden. Thus in Christianity it represents temptation, the loss of Eden and of innocence. It can therefore symbolise guilt and shame on your part.

In Greek mythology, it represents love and desire. People that doodle apples are likely to be naughty, and delight in the more sensual aspects of life.

Also see: Food

Arrows

Arrows represent direction and ambition. There are many different types of arrows which indicate different traits.

A broken arrow signals a disappointment in love or work.

An arrow drawn with a heart is cupid's arrow —you are a hopeless romantic.

An arrow pointing at an object represents frustration.

An arrow pointing at or running through a person represents anger and aggression.

If the arrow is drawn in an outline and pointing upwards, you have a strong drive to progress or better yourself.

If the arrow has many heads, it expresses a persistent personality, who never gives up. If the arrow has two heads that point in opposite directions it shows that you are unconvinced or undecided about a particular subject.

If the arrow is shaded then it may indicate hesitancy about making a decision.

If you draw many arrows all pointing in the same direction it means your are extremely ambitious, but are a little undecided on what exactly you are to do next.

Arrows drawn pointing in lots of different directions means you have lots of creative juices. You might have so many good ideas that you're just not sure what to do with them all.

ANALYSING YOUR DOODLES

Baby

A doodle of a baby can represent curiosity, joy, a new phase of life, a new idea. Often the baby represents a part of your personality or a talent that has not had the chance to express itself and develop. It can also signal requited love. These doodles usually mean you are a gentle, romantic person who has a love of children.

Drawing crying babies suggests that there is some ill health in your family, or it may denote some sort of disappointment you've had recently.

Badger

The term 'badgering' someone may apply if you draw these self-sufficient, yet aggressive animals. You may feel as if you want to escape from other people's company and influences as you feel hassled and unable to cope with mounting pressures.

Indeed you may want to mimic the secluded life of the badger and take some time out to be on your own.

If the badger has sharp, spiky fur, it can show that you are feeling defensive and spiky yourself. If the fur is rounded, it shows that you are a caring person, who probably loves animals.

Bag and suitcase

A bag represents your emotional 'baggage' — be it from failed relationships or disillusion-ment. It holds all those ideas, beliefs, grudges and information you carry around with you but would rather drop. The bag symbolises a desire to forget the past, change your tired attitudes and move on to something new.

The 'hangbag', in particular, is an expres-sion of your own identity, everything you need is in your handbag. Maybe you think you've got your life sewn up and your identity or image is clear in your mind. A closed suitcase which features a lock, shows you are in denial about certain issues. Your longings and fears have long been repressed. The suitcase is also a symbol of status and independence. It can show a strong desire for change and some kind of journey (physical and metaphorical) may be about to commence.

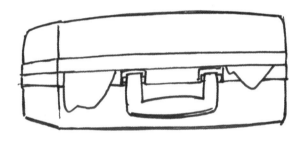

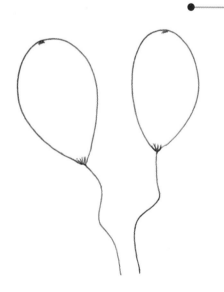

Balloon

A balloon either reveals a desire to be a child again, or it shows that you still possess the innocence of a child. The release of a balloon into the air demonstrates hope. It may be that you are in the process of testing an idea out and hoping that it flies.

The release of a balloon may also symbolise the letting go of something or of someone. It expresses freedom and the idea of fate taking its course.

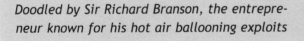

Doodled by Sir Richard Branson, the entrepreneur known for his hot air ballooning exploits

British actor Greg Wise doodled a monkey holding balloons with faces

Bat

The bat has a number of associations. It can be an expression of a highly intuitive individual — reflecting an ability to see in the dark.

However, the bat is also associated with vampires and blood-suckers. It may represent a fear of your repressed fears that lie in your unconscious.

It is also a symbol of the spirit of death in some cultures, and may therefore signal that you are thinking of your own mortality and what death means to you. Otherwise, you may have someone close that is in bad health.

Bath

If you draw baths you could have a strong desire to be cleansed of something. It may be that you want to rid yourself of guilt of some sort and want to 'come clean'. It represents a change of heart where old ways are altered for the better.

The bath or bathing can be seen as a ritual that is getting you ready for something big that's about to happen to you. It may be that you are about to face up to your fears about your relationships. It shows a desire to share something and open up to someone close to you. Once you share your secret with someone, your life may change dramatically.

Beach

The beach symbolises a relaxed state of mind. It can signal that you are open to new life experiences. A beach which shows the ocean in the background indicates a day dreamer. You are also a romantic with a huge heart. Your reflectiveness and quietness can sometimes be mistaken for aloofness.

Also see: Sea, Island and Water

Bear

A bear is either thought of as a loveable, huggable cuddly toy, or as a ferocious threatening wild animal. Depending on how you draw bears — as threatening? or as cuddly toys? — you either feel threatened and in danger, or you have a desire to be loved.

The bear can also represent competition. You may feel threatened by someone at work or you feel you are trying to compete with someone's affections. Dancing bears? Drawing a dancing bear reveals a cheeky, mischievous humour.

Bed

A clean, well-made bed indicates that you are at peace with yourself. It may indicate the presence of a new lover and a positive new force in your life.

You tend to love comfort, luxury and lounging. The bed is where you meet your unconscious in the form of dreams. Therefore, doodling beds may indicate a desire to get to know yourself better and to find out what's locked away in the depths of your unconscious. If the bed is outside, it shows a desire for new adventures.

Bee

Bees by nature are hard-working, and work collectively within their bee community. Hence the expression 'busy bee'. You may draw a bee because you like the uniformity of the black and yellow lines on the bee's body. In this case you tend to be someone who keeps your cool in emergencies. You are able to concentrate and you know what you want from life.

Bees also invoke images of sweetness and honey. The bee doodle indicates a warm-hearted, gentle person who is a romantic.

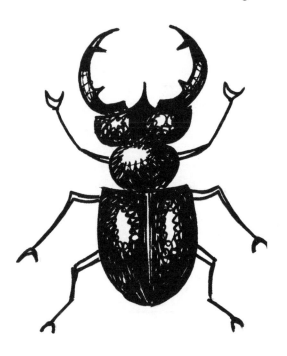

Beetle

A beetle, with the exception of the ladybird, is usually a dirty, ugly creature. The beetle would be the baddy in a film. Beetles suggest that you feel sex is dirty. You may feel ashamed about your sexuality.

As well as a possible disdain for intimacy and sex, you might feel powerless and insignificant (among the swarm).

Alternatively, you could be being plagued by something or someone, whom you would rather just got lost. In folklore certain beetles if trodden on can bring rain, which may be good or bad luck.

Beer glass

A beer glass usually indicates that you are a very gregarious person, who loves the sensual pleasures of life.

If the glass is drawn in a three-dimensional form, it would suggest that you are extremely organised, and good at planning. You are likely to draw other three-dimensional shapes such as cones and cubes, showing the presence of a creative eye, and practical mindedness.

Also see: Shapes

Bell

A doorbell indicates desiring something or someone new in your life. It says: 'you can ring my bell anytime, now, soon, some time this century, PLEASE!!' type attitude. A swinging bell shows you are governed by time in an obsessive way — you are always punctual and impatient with others who do not have the same outlook.

A doodle of a bell can also signal that you have just had some success, usually in a professional capacity. You want to shout your latest success from the rooftops. You have a larger than life personality and you're not afraid of saying exactly what you think.

Bicycle

Bicycle doodles reveal an anticipation that something lucky is about to happen to you. You may be a lover of nature and of cycling itself. You tend to be active in all areas of your life and your hard work almost always pays off in the end. You are forever going on exciting excursions and involving other people in your endeavours.

For many, learning to ride a bicycle is something unforgettable, like a baby's first steps. It represents learning a new skill and gaining freedom. Remember the patience and confidence you needed for your first solo bike ride? You probably exhibit the very same traits or you have a desire to mirror these traits in your life now.

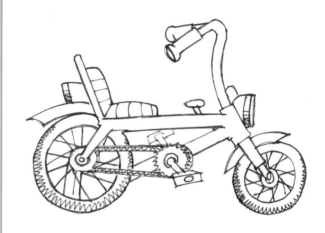

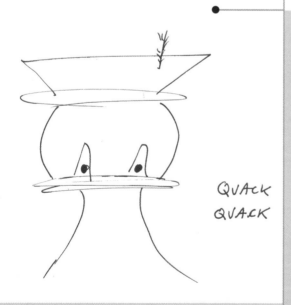

QUACK
QUACK

British author Dick Francis doodles a cartoon bird with a hat, indicating strong beliefs

Birds

Doodles of birds flying show imagination, intuition, unconscious passions, and a desire for freedom. They may also represent a desire to connect to your spiritual side. A dove symbolises peace and is therefore associated with a happy, caring, loving person. An owl is the symbol of wisdom. You are all-seeing and usually a loner. An eagle shows you have a sense of pride, and sometimes arrogant tendencies, but above all you are a survivor. A hen may allude to a feeling of being hen-pecked in a relationship. A cock reflects a protective and confident type of person. A swan symbolises elegance, grace and regality.

Eminent artist Ralph Steadman doodles a big bird in boots, taking big strides in life

British actress and politician Glenda Jackson draws swans, symbolising grace and regality

Author Louis de Bernieres doodles a house as a bird, suggesting a roaming existence

Boat/ship/yacht

A boat represents you — its body symbolises the parts of your personality that have allowed you to survive your journey through life. Your head is above water — you are a survivor.

It also symbolises a desire for adventure and you are likely to be a day dreamer. Boats tend to be drawn on oceans or ponds. They are usually positive symbols unless they are shown overturned or under water.

If the boat is drawn floating on water it also represents a vessel that is difficult to escape from. You may feel that you have certain bonds or commitments that are not easy to break away from.

The condition of the boat itself is an expression of your physical self. Are you taking good care of yourself? Are you burning the candle at both ends?

Your boat can represent a refuge for all the worries and burdens of life. It is a place of safety and tranquillity. If the doodle is of a person disembarking, it represents leaving behind a particular phase of your life be it a job, motherhood etc.

If there is a person embarking, it shows you are a solitary sort of person who is either a loner naturally or is feeling lonely at the moment.

If the boat is drawn with a moon in the background (i.e. it is night time) it represents the desire to find your roots.

Bomb

This suggests the presence of aggression in your life. You may feel that there is hostility aimed at you or that you have a desire to be aggressive towards someone else. The bomb can also represent a fear of death.

Book

A book represents all the memories, things you have learned and experiences in your life. It is about you, your life and of knowledge. It can also signal a thirst for more knowledge and learning.

Bottle

If the bottle is empty this is a good sign. You are adept at overcoming hurdles in your life and are open to new possibilities.

If the bottle contains something, it can signify that you are feeling restricted in a certain area of your life. You are literally feeling 'bottled up'.

A bottle of wine can represent an urge to share something important with someone else, and a desire to bond with someone be it at work or with a loved one.

Box

These types of doodles are very common. Generally a box or cube can be a reflection of memories or treasured experiences. An interpretation of the doodle will depend on the type of box.

An open box may show a desire to welcome someone new into your life. Or it may represent a desire to escape from a restrictive situation. Stacked boxes represent a methodical, logical thinker.

A closed box means you have a tendency to be self-centred. You are also a private person and don't tolerate interfering people. You are methodical and practical.

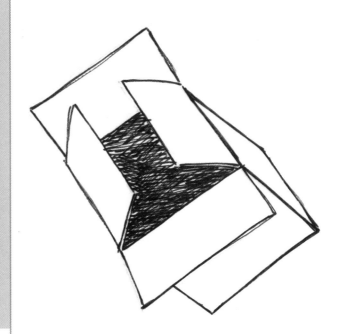

Brick wall

A brick wall is another common doodle which can either be viewed as a number of rectangles or a number of symmetrical horizontal and vertical lines. The symmetry of the lines shows you are logical, practical and stable. You are also well-grounded and have a straightforward approach to life. You are serious about relationships and usually have long-term aspirations.

A brick wall can also represent the opposite of the above and shows a desire to cut yourself off from the outside world.

Bricks in themselves can sometimes denote unsettled business or love affairs.

Breasts

If you scribble breasts, it is possible that it represents sexual desire and fantasy, however, it is more likely to be an unconscious expression of the feminine soul, or 'anima'. Men who do these doodles exhibit extremely masculine traits, but their corresponding anima (which is hidden) is predominantly feminine.

If a female doodler draws breasts it is likely that she is more interested in motherhood rather than sexual desire.

It may also represent a need to return to infantile dependency. You no longer want to accept the responsibilities of adulthood and want to be taken care of by someone else.

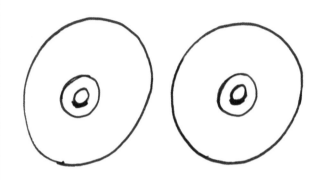

Bridge

The bridge represents a vision of how to overcome an obstacle or hurdle in your life. It can also represent a transition in your life.

You may find that you are entering a new phase of your life and the bridge represents the link between self and opportunity/change.

It can also represent maturity. You are growing up, and about to leave your youth behind.

Whatever transition you are experiencing, the bridge is a symbol that you know, perhaps unconsciously, that the other side is full of hope. You are at a crossroads in your life but optimistic about the future.

THE SCIENCE & PSYCHOLOGY OF

Broom

A broom doodle has various interpretations. It can reveal a feeling of regret about something, the broom representing a desire to sweep everything under the carpet. Alternatively, a broom in flight is a magical kind of object associated with witches and wizards. It can indicate you have an interest in the paranormal and occult. It also suggests you are a daydreamer, with your head in the clouds.

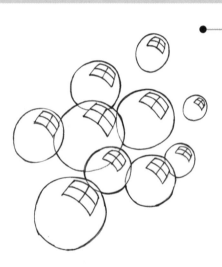

Bubbles

Forever drawing bubbles may signify that unless you do something about your dreams, they will never materialise. Each bubble signifies another forgotten daydream.

You tend to be highly creative and full of entrepreneurial ideas. But unless you take a risk you will always feel unsatisfied in your life.

Bus

A bus indicates the frustration of getting from 'a' to 'b', both physically and metaphorically, and having to depend on others to get there.

It can also reveal the need for you to gain new experiences and share them with a group of people. You are sure to be very sociable, and love going to parties. However, you may not be too sure about how to cope with problems on your own.

Bull

The bull is a symbol of the power of healing and fertility. The bull is also a very macho symbol. Men that doodle bulls are probably trying to prove themselves sexually or feel they need to dominate their partner.

Female doodlers may feel that they are being dominated by their partner and they feel ambivalent to being the object of domination.

In either case, you may feel the need to release some sort of repressed anger.

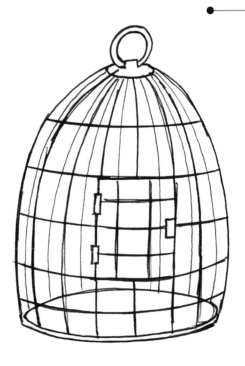

Cage

You feel a sense of frustration — social pressures may be restraining you from being able to freely express yourself. You may feel that your job or your relationship is suffocating and you feel trapped.

Doodling a cage is a way of expressing how you imprison yourself with anger, resentment and depression. Or you may feel trapped by a childhood trauma that you have not yet come to terms with.

Whatever the circumstances, unless you find an outlet for the frustration, you may continue to suffer emotionally, which can have long-lasting effects.

Calendar

To doodle a calendar indicates that you are a very orderly, methodical type of person. You are probably someone whose habits die hard. You are also someone who is conscious of the passage of time.

If you always doodle the same date in a calender it can signify that something important happened in your life on this date. It is usually an expression of regret, even if the date is associated with good memories.

If the specific date doesn't ring a bell, look at what you associate with each individual month, day or year as this may give you some clue as to why the numbers are significant.

Camel

The camel is associated with aridness. This may be a dry patch in your life i.e. you don't have the sense that your life is progressing, you feel apathetic and lack drive. This lack of feeling may mean you are overwhelmed by the responsibilities and difficulties your life brings you.

However, just as the camel carries water reserves in its hump, so you also have the wherewithal to get through this difficult period. By trying to bring your usual patience and perseverance to the fore, which you possess in abundance, you can overcome virtually anything.

Candle

A candle represents life. It suggests that you are feeling vulnerable and are looking at the meaning of life and mortality. You are perhaps at a junction in your life where you feel that you have been successful in most things, but somehow there is still something missing, or which doesn't yet make sense.

It is possible, therefore, that this is the time to embark on a spiritual journey to gain further awareness of yourself, and attain what Jung called a true 'personality'. This is a soul searching period for you. This will be a difficult journey, but afterwards you'll have a greater understanding of the world.

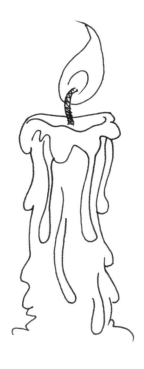

Cards

Playing cards represents a sense of fate, and a life of chance. They are an indication that there is something out of balance in your personality or life. You need to discover what is troubling you in order to be able to reach some equilibrium and inner calm.

The suit of the cards you doodle determines the area of your life you may be experiencing problems with.

Hearts: emotions, relationships, love.
Diamonds: finances, intellect.
Spades: sensuality, health.
Clubs: sex, responsibility, work.

Car

A doodle of a car represents sex, ambition and motivation. The car gives us the ability to move around and symbolises the power we have to succeed in our own lives, to make choices and achieve results. It shows you feel in charge of your own destiny.

Does your car have a driver? The driver represents you, your independent streak and unhesitant decision-making. It can also suggest that you are tackling problems on your own. You may find it difficult to share.

Do you draw cars with passengers? This indicates that you are thinking of those important in your life or people that have an influence over you.

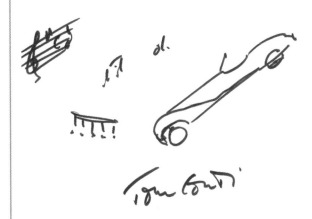

Footballer Wayne Bridge's doodle of a car, symbolic of a drive to succeed	Actor Tom Conti's doodle of a car – a symbol of sex, ambition and motivation

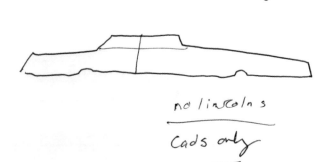

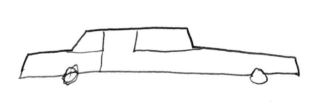

Cat

The cat is often seen as a source of comfort and affection. For some women it can represent a substitute baby and can therefore represent an urge to care for someone or have a baby of your own. If you are a male doodler of cats, it shows you to be in tune with your feminine side. You are very intuitive.

The cat can also represent a deep psychological secret, possibly an undiscovered part of your nature.

You tend to be very generous, warm and caring. You will always be a loyal friend.

Author Maeve Binchy's doodle of a cat — symbolic of generosity and warmth

Actress Brenda Blethyn's doodle of a talking cat, representing intuition

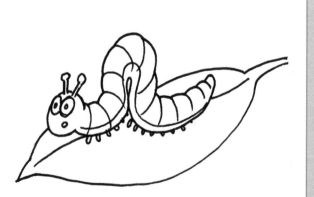

Caterpillar

It may be that you are experiencing or about to experience major changes in your life. You are evolving both psychologically and emotionally — you are, in essence, maturing. This is a time to work on your personal development. It may mean you need to take some time out to do this. Surround yourself by nature, away from the city, it may do you the world of good.

Cemetery/gravestone/coffin

Continually doodling funeral paraphernalia shows a preoccupation with death. Ask yourself how you perceive death.

Do you perceive death as a neutralisation of time? As a sense of wholeness and completeness? Or is your doodle a way of looking at life and death as part of a meaningful totality? Do you view death as 'nothingness' or death as 'presence'?

It could be that you've just experienced a bereavement and you are reflecting on what death means to you.

It is possible that you feel some kind of resentment or bitterness about the death or

loss of something or someone who was an important and integral part of your life?

You may be preoccupied with thoughts of a former relationship that is now 'dead and buried' and you are looking to the future, a new phase, a new birth. Death is associated with birth and sexuality. So it does not have to have negative associations.

If you draw a coffin, you have a strong sense of your own mortality. You may be examining your feelings about your own mortality or of someone else's.

As well as reflecting on what death means to you, you may be scared of losing someone close or you are anxious about health-related matters.

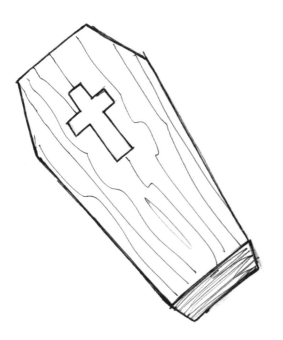

Chain

You may feel restricted and imprisoned. It is often the case that you feel trapped in a relationship or in your chosen career. You may also feel trapped by attitudes or habits. The links in the chain are of significance, they represent links in a series of events that have led to the present.

If you draw yourself shackled in chains, it suggests that you are feeling overburdened and stressed. Alternatively, it may have sexual overtones, suggesting a sado-masochistic tendency.

Chairs

A doodle of a chair means you have failed to meet some obligation. It represents passivity. You probably have a relaxed attitude to your life and your commitments.

This is a trait that can frustrate others you come into contact with. People may question your reliability and integrity. This can mean you will run the risk of alienating yourself and losing friends.

Also see: Table

Church

The church tends to be a symbol of peace. It is a place you wish to be — at peace with yourself. You may be trying to resolve some emotional problems in your life.

Alternatively, you may be thinking about spirituality and religion. You are seeking solace and protection.

Also see: Houses/Buildings

Cigar/cigarette/pipe

For the smoker it represents a conscious desire to light up, but an unconscious expression of guilt. It may represent a wish to return to infantile dependency. You literally want to return to sucking on your mother's breast.

It can also be interpreted as a phallic symbol and symbolises repressed sexual desires. Showing someone smoking a cigarette, cigar or pipe infers a desire for a kiss or oral sex.

Cigarette lighter

Doodling cigarette lighters generally signals that you are constantly thinking about sex. You are probably a big flirt and attracted to short-term relationships.

Circles and mandalas

Circles

The circle is an extremely important doodle. It represents your quest to find wholeness, unity and peace. The circle, according to Jung, represents your soul. You are on the right path to balancing all the parts of your psyche, both conscious and unconscious. If you believe you are a certain personality type which stems from the four functions of the psyche — thinking, feeling, sensation and intuition — you are endeavouring to reconcile all of these functions. You are striving to clear up conflict, you are attempting unification of the male and female elements of your psyche,

and you strive for a union of opposites. You may be on a spiritual journey, and you are willing to confront your unconscious head on. You are closer than ever to achieving real 'personality' and finding your true self.

You are likely to be an honest, loving individual. Your quest for self-knowledge is also a desire to be strong enough to care and support others close to you in your life. Repeated circles in an orderly straight line show you to be cautious in your judgment of others, and patient when approaching tasks. Circles within circles show you may be under pressure and you feel the need to withdraw defensively. Circles that are very sketchy and weak represent a lack of concentration — you are too distracted to be able to cope with the task that lies before you.

Mandalas

The Sanskrit word 'mandala' means circle. In religion and psychology it represents circular images, which are drawn, painted, modelled or danced. Mandalas are said to represent the union of the four elements which are forever tending to fall apart.

Modern mandalas come in the form of snakes, suns, flowers, stars, globes, crosses etc. and all symbolise the centre of ourselves. Jung interpreted his own drawings of mandalas, which became central to his teachings. He saw the mandala as the centre of being, the exponent of all paths, the path to the centre, to individuation.

March 26 2003 4:30 p.m.

Actress Gillian Anderson's doodle is reminiscent of some of Jung's mandalas

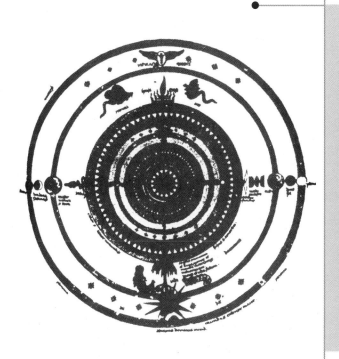

"My mandalas were cryptograms concerning the state of the self which were presented to me anew each day. In them I saw the self — that is, my whole being — actively at work. To be sure, at first I could only dimly understand them; but they seemed to me highly significant, and I guarded them like precious pearls. I had the distinct feeling that they were something central, and in time I acquired through them a living conception of the self. The self, I thought, was like the monad which I am, and which is my world. The mandala represents this monad, and corresponds to the microcosmic nature of the psyche." Jung

THE SCIENCE & PSYCHOLOGY OF

Cliff

A doodle of a cliff usually signifies that you are about to take a big risk or change your life radically. You could be looking at death straight in the face and you're either going to jump or make the positive decision that's about to change your life forever.

Clock

People who draw clocks tend to have an enormous sense of duty. They are also acutely aware of how short life is and they are keen not to waste any time. These people tend to enjoy a very full, satisfying life.

Clothes

Clothes represent how you hide the real you behind a protective shield. It's a defence from the outside world and other people. They symbolise the attitude we take with us when meeting people or approaching new situations. Drawing clothes may reflect your need to deflect feelings of shyness, anxiety or nervousness.

Clothes are an expression of a worry of how you come across or are perceived by other people. Drawing underwear may mean you are expressing your sexual desires. Drawing a shirt or blouse means you are acutely aware of your public image. A dress represents a strong sense of your own femininity.

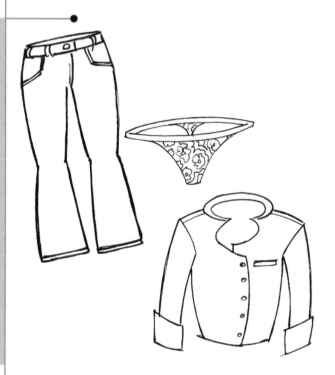

Clouds

Fluffy, happy clouds indicate you are a warm-hearted person who is a bit of a daydreamer. You also have a sense of freedom about you.

Angry, shaded, rain clouds indicate that you could be going through a period of depression, or that you are feeling a huge burden on your shoulders. It may be that life has dealt you a bad hand, and you are finding it difficult to cope.

Drawing clouds generally has a therapeutic affect on you. Their billowy, soft, cotton wool like texture lends itself to a freedom of expression. You do not have an obsessive nature, instead you are pretty easy-going.

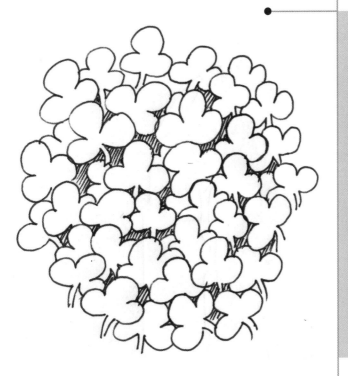

Clover

Drawing a clover leaf denotes an optimist with a thirst and enthusiasm for life. You feel your dreams are being fulfiled and there are no hurdles that can't be overcome.

You tend to be compassionate, loyal and faithful, and you are interested only in long-term partnerships.

Sometimes you are highly idealistic, which means if things don't go to plan, you can feel devastated. But when life runs smoothly your enthusiasm is almost infectious.

The clover leaf also represents fertility and can signify that you are thinking about pregnancy and childbirth.

Computer

Doodles of computers show you are interested in technology, and highly organised. The computer represents an outlet to the outside world. It represents endless possibilities, interactions with other people, and a resource of information.

It symbolises a person with a thirst for knowledge. You are probably a quick learner and keen to interact with other like-minded people. You may also be a lover of science fiction, and would make a god inventor.

Cow

The cow is a sacred animal in India. You may draw a cow in homage to this spiritual animal, which implies you are either religious or you are respectful of other religions and customs.

It is also an ancient symbol of motherhood. You probably have a strong bond with your mother. You may be quite maternal and are good at caring for others.

Crab

The crab indicates you are a very guarded person. You protect yourself with a seemingly hard exterior but underneath you are a very sensitive soul. You are likely to be very defensive. Anyone who crosses you will forever find a grudge being harboured against them.

Your defence shell makes you difficult to get to know, but once you do allow someone in you will give them the world.

Colours

Usually doodles are penned in whatever coloured pen is at hand, but some people do purposely choose a variety of colours.

Red represents power. It can also indicate anger or a need to impose authority. In China, red is the colour of prosperity and joy.

Blue, black and grey indicate stability and strength.

Green and blue are related to water and the sea.

Purple may represent sexual frustration or a need to appear unorthodox. Historically, purple has represented royalty, and in darker hues suggests magic and mystery.

A preference for brown can indicate a conservative, even repressed person.

Green is usually regarded as a restful, calm colour and is favoured by well balanced individuals.

Cup

The cup signifies that you are open to the possibility of love and sexuality. It may mean you would leap at the chance of jumping into bed with a new man/woman in your life.

In relationships you are usually broad-minded sexually. You are sensual and very warm-hearted. You also tend to be sincere, loyal and highly intuitive emotionally.

Also see: Beer mug

Cupid

Amor, amor, amor... You are a sentimental, romantic. You have either already found love and happiness or you are desperately looking for it. You live for love above all other desires and will stop at nothing to find the person that can bring your dreams to fruition.

When in a relationship you may be jealous and possessive, and often you find yourself fighting for your lover's affections.

The cupid can also be a symbol of unrequited love. So, you might be reflecting heavily on someone who has turned his/her back on you. It may be time to move on and look to the future.

Deer

The deer means you are very sensitive to criticism from others. You are likely to be very caring, gentle and warm-hearted. Your vulnerability could lead others to take advantage of you. The deer can also symbolise lovesickness.

If you draw reindeers, you are likely to be thinking about familial relationships. This kind of doodle evokes images of Christmas and festivities, in which family is at the forefront of your thoughts.

Doodles of deers with huge antlers can have phallic overtones. In this case it can represent fertility and may indicate some sexual repression and frustration.

Desk

It is likely that you are concentrating on an important project at the moment. The desk is a symbol of work, discipline and communication.

You are a practical minded person who is excellent at working through things in a methodical way. You also display the potential to be good with your hands. You are probably handy around the house or good at constructing things.

The desk itself, if drawn symmetrically, shows you are methodical and efficient, which is an excellent asset in your chosen career. Your fastidiousness is such that you sometimes forget to let your hair down.

Devil

Drawing devils, demons or gargoyles represents emotions or urges that you don't feel entirely in control of, or that are being repressed. The urges may be so strong that they are controlling you, so you show them in the form of an external force. The urges are ones you do not want to have and therefore they represent an enemy or an evil – in this case the devil.

The devil can also represent some form of repressed guilt, sometimes associated with repressed sexual desires. This may also represent your desire to find balance in your psyche, an attempt to resolve conflict.

Dice

While you may be connected to the gambling world in some way, or be attracted to risk-taking, you are more likely to be attracted to the shape of the dice itself, rather than the games it is associated with.

A cube says you are a practical, efficient person who is focused on what you want to achieve in life. You are a great planner and meticulous in everything you do. The circles within the cube are neatly ordered and suggest you have the same orderly approach to life.

It is more likely that it is the dice's shape that is relevant, and is less to do with chance and luck. However, if you are attracted to the world of gambling, you'll be sure to weigh up all the eventualities before placing bets.

Dog

If you draw dogs, you may be seeking reassurance in love. Your dog may have been the only source of demonstrative love during your childhood, so the symbol of the dog represents this. You may be feeling lonely and in need of affection. You are likely to be an animal lover, have a caring side and are very loyal in relationships. A black dog can signal depression or a fear of death. A dog bearing his teeth means someone is either attacking or criticising you. A dog on a lead represents the feeling that you are being stopped from expressing yourself fully. It also suggests feelings about wanting a child or the need for love.

ANALYSING YOUR DOODLES

British actress Julie Walters of Educating Rita fame draws a hairy mutt, showing sensitivity

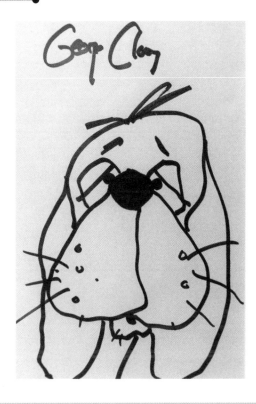

Actor George Clooney's doodle of a dog shows his love of animals and caring side

Doll

Doodling a doll may show that you are thinking about events in your childhood. It could be that the doll symbolises a traumatic childhood — maybe you were smacked as a child or emotionally attacked and the doll represents a child unable to fight back.

Also, it shows a desire to be idolised and loved, or to feel valued in some way. It can also be evidence of someone who loves children.

Dolphin

The dolphin is a symbol of guidance and protection. You either feel the need to be protected or you are presently caring for a loved one. You have a sensitive nature and you hold honesty important in relationships. You are also likely to be a lover of animals and nature. You are good at communicating, particularly with children.

Donkey

The donkey can represent your plodding, long suffering body. It can be an expression of the relationship you have with your body's needs and impulses. You may be the kind of person who lives on whims or fancies. You are prone to stubbornness like the donkey itself. Perhaps you have habits which you find hard to break. You're sure as hell not going to be the one to admit to being in the wrong when you have an argument with your partner. If you draw someone else pulling or riding the donkey, you may be feeling that you are doing all the work in a relationship. If the person riding the donkey is you, then it could mean you are feeling in an inferior position in a relationship.

Dragon

Historically dragons are slain to gain treasure or fair maidens. Dragons represent the monstrous fear of the unconscious and the slaying of dragons could represent a successful taming of overpowering sexual urges. It may also represent the fear of a particularly aggressive person, perhaps a mother or father figure. There is an element of underlying fear in terms of self-control, anger that has been suppressed and an overwhelming terror of death. If the dragon drawn has wings an escape from these fears is possible through self-belief and self-knowledge. As dramatic as these interpretations are in the West, in the East the dragon symbolises good fortune and luck. An Eastern doodler may simply be representing an unconscious request for luck or even some kind of spiritual enlightenment.

Earrings

Earrings, and jewellery in general, represent something of value. If the earrings drawn were received as a gift, then the doodle is an expression of your feelings about the person who has given them.

It could also represent something valuable in the sense of your quality of life. It may symbolise that you are thinking about something you have learned to value over the years — it may not be something material but could represent friendships, and bonds with your family.

Egg

The egg symbolises new birth — perhaps a part of yourself, a hidden talent for example, is getting ready to materialise. It can also represent a desire to settle down, nest and have a family.

Elephant

The elephant is a powerful, dominant animal. It can symbolise inner strength and usually shows that you can overcome any hurdle. An elephant is usually drawn as a friendly creature, which reflects your own character traits. You are likely to be a bit of a joker, mischievous, social and a joy to be around.

Eyes

Doodles of eyes often show the inner self of the doodler. Huge eyes indicate that you have a big personality and a sensitive nature. Small eyes show you are introverted and reserved. Closed eyes indicate introversion and hesitance about looking deep into yourself.

Does the expression of the eye indicate anything? Do the eyes look frightened, sad, happy? This is also likely to be an insight into your inner self. If you draw expressive eyes, you are likely to be acutely self-aware and extremely perceptive.

Zoologist and British TV presenter Desmond Morris's doodle of surreal eyes

Face

The expression on the face, as well as its angle, shows a lot about you. A face drawn face-on and not in profile shows you to be gregarious and extrovert. You need to be in a job in which you can communicate with other people. You are likely to have a network of close friends. If the doodle of the face is huge then it shows you to be over-confident with a rather arrogant air. A tiny face can mean you feel vulnerable, and perhaps insecure about your looks or your intellectual prowess. If the face drawn is unhappy it is clearly a stressful period for you and you are less than optimistic. In contrast, a happy or smiling face reveals your fun-loving side and sense of humour. Ugly or angry-looking

faces show that you currently lack any passion for life. You are disillusioned and your anger is hard to disguise. A surprised face (raised eyebrows for example) show you need to control a situation that has got out of hand. A beautiful face shows you are loving and caring. You are optimistic about the future and do not have many conscious insecurities.

Mouths: The mouth is important in the face doodle — does it show fangs or sharp teeth? This indicates anger. Is it large and open? You probably like to be the centre of attention. Does the face have a big grin? This represents your inability to reveal the 'real you' to others, instead you put on a show. A small mouth shows you are tight-lipped, reserved and not used to gossiping. Missing teeth signals decay or even death. You know that life is short and that you need to get on with it before it's too late.

Noses: In folklore, the size of the nose was said to relate to the size of a man's penis. If you are a male doodler and always draw large noses on your faces, it is likely that you are either very proud of the assets that you have been endowed with or you dream of being better equipped. If you draw a face without a nose it may show you are embarrassed about your own sexuality. If you are a female doodler and you draw a hooked or noticeably droopy nose it may indicate dissatisfaction with your partner. If the nose is rounded, you have an open attitude towards sex and are happy in your love life.

Chin/jawline: A very angular jawline shows you are domineering and confident. A rounder chin shows you to be more laid back in your attitude to others. A long, narrow chin shows you to be

A doodle by Uri Geller, paranormal expert, of two faces in profile

a little withdrawn and reserved.

Eyelashes: Long eyelashes are evidence of a vanity. If you are a male doodler, it reveals your strong feminine side.

Eyebrows: Very thick, unruly eyebrows indicate that you feel your life is getting out of hand. You are creative and need some way of bringing order. Raised eyebrows show that you need to exercise control. Thin, neat eyebrows show you like order and efficiency

Ear: The size of the ear shows how receptive you are to others and how good you are at giving advice. Large ears show you are willing to listen. Small ears shows you have selfish tendencies.

Neck: A short neck indicates you are not open or receptive to others. A long neck shows you are forever challenging yourself and determined.

Feather

Generally a feather indicates a whimsical nature, with a cheeky sort of humour. What type of feather is it? An eagle's feather for instance shows you are proud, protective and dominant.

A peacock's feather shows you have an awareness of spirituality. You tend to be unconcerned with material possessions, and more concerned with how we might be governed by the movements of the planets.

A black feather would indicate you are keen to explore the workings of your unconscious mind.

A white feather suggests that you are aspirational.

Feet and footsteps

Drawing feet means you are imbued with a sense of dominance and power. The Hindu god Vishnu took three footsteps which covered the whole universe. When Puss in Boots took one step it covered a vast area. Feet and footsteps symbolise that you are aspirational, taking big strides in your life. You are ready to take on the world. Drawing feet may also represent a desire to go walkabout, and return to nature. You may be feeling restless and need to have a temporary change of scene.

Or else, you may associate feet with the phrase 'to put one's foot in it'. A recent faux pas may have left you feeling guilty.

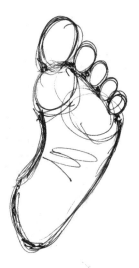

Fire

Fire can represent passion, sexuality and desire. Your personality can show all the above traits. You are likely to be a very romantic, sensual and great lover.

Fire, however, is also harmful and destructive. Therefore it may represent a fierce, angry temperament. It is also an expression of an internal force that gives us vitality.

Fish

For the early Christians the fish was a symbol of the regeneration of mankind. Your doodle shows you are letting feelings emerge that have not previously been released. As these new feelings come to the fore, a new sense of the self emerges. It is a sign of personal growth. The fish is also a symbol of fertility. Groups of little fish can symbolise sperm, which represent our journeys through life.

Flag

A flag denotes pride either of your own or nationalistic pride. It is also an expression of victory or a form of rejoicing. A shaded flag: you are feeling anxious and under pressure either because of work or for personal reasons. A chequered flag: the black and white squares of the flag show some conflict in your life that needs resolving. A square flag: you are practical, methodical and stable. You possess a lot of common sense and you are down to earth.

THE SCIENCE & PSYCHOLOGY OF

Flowers

If you draw flowers, you tend to be a happy-go-lucky individual with a warm heart. You are always keen to help others out. You are sentimental, romantic, and faithful when in a relationship.

The flower may also represent the blossoming of personal qualities, love, or children. Flowers in bloom signify pleasure.

Withered flowers suggest you are in a gloomy place, or have been disappointed recently.

Doodlers of flowers tend to be full of energy and cheerfulness, qualities that will help you to be happy in life.

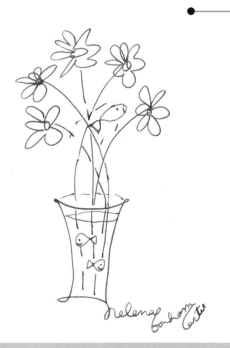

British actress Helena Bonham-Carter draws flowers and fish, signs of life and fertility

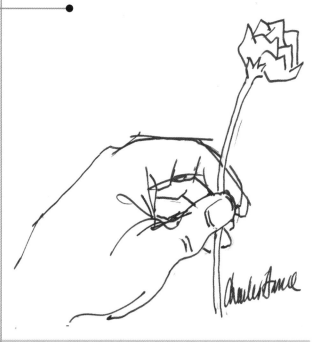

British actor Charles Dance doodles a hand and a flower, showing energy and confidence

Forest

Trees are commonly featured in mythology and religious scripts (see Trees), and are thus very significant. A forest has a slightly different meaning to an individual tree doodle. It represents a deep awareness of the unconscious. The forest is associated with magic, mysticism, elves and fairies.

It is likely that you have something buried deep in your unconscious, possibly a secret that you have carried with you for years but which now feels a burden. Also, the forest is associated with survival. Whatever is being repressed, may impede your survival, in an emotional and physical sense.

Fountain

The fountain is a symbol of life and vitality. You are living every minute of your life for the moment and enjoying it immensely, radiating joy and optimism. It also reveals you are a very giving sort of individual who realises how precious life is.

The fountain also signals birth, renewal and regeneration. Like holy water that might be used to baptise a baby, the fountain represents a more advanced stage of your life. This may be the time when striving to find your true self is of utmost importance. It could reveal that the best part of your life is just around the corner.

Food

Doodling food demonstrates that you have a great capacity for sensuality. It shows you are fully embracing life, absorbing experiences and feeling greater for it.

Food can represent the nourishment that you feel is necessary to lead a full life, this is not food nourishment but the nourishment of life events and relationships. You are likely to have a high sex drive and often think erotic thoughts.

Fruit represents sensuality. Soft squidgy fruit such as peaches represent the female genitalia. Long fruits such as bananas depict male sexuality and the phallus. Grapes reveal

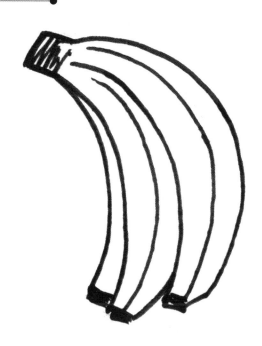

you to be sensual, decadent and sexually driven. You can become pre-disposed to jealousy in close personal relationships. An apple represents temptation and the consequences if temptation overcomes. Lemons show bitterness and malice.

Vegetables symbolise basic needs and a contented material satisfaction. Carrots are phallic. Onions imply sadness. To draw cake, sweets or candy reveals sensuality, a love of pleasure and special intimate friendships.

Also see: Phallic symbols

Frog

The frog represents transformation. It expresses a desire on your part for personal development. You may be feeling self-conscious about your looks and feel the need to change your outward appearance.

Games

Doodling games shows an element of fear or anxiety that is usually related to business or love. You may be predisposed to gambling and competitiveness. You either take winning and losing very seriously, or on the other hand you view life in a light-hearted way — seeing it as if it were playing a game — 'you win some, you lose some' kind of attitude.

Chessboards
The doodling of chessboards represents the polarity of the human psyche, and of pairs of opposites such as: chaos and order, good and evil, odd and even. There may be some

conflict in your life that you are trying to solve, and there's a battle taking place in your unconscious. It can also represent a desire for success and the ups and downs you have on the way to achieving your goal.

Snakes and ladders
The game 'snakes and ladders' reveals you to be an ambitious person who is striving to reach the top of your career.

Number boards
A number board demonstrates the need for facts. You are financially ambitious and mathematically skilled.

Dartboards
A dartboard is a collection of lines, and circles within circles. The circle itself is an expression of wholeness and a desire to be rounded

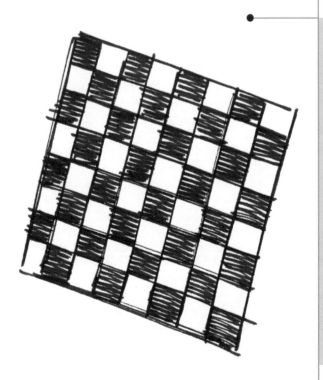

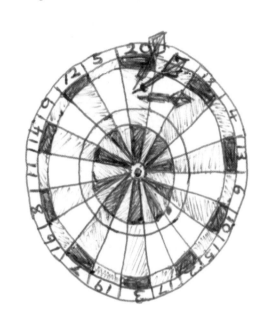

psychologically. Circles within circles generally represent someone who feels vulnerable and wants protecting. In the game itself there is a sense of risk or achievement.

The presence of numbers on the dartboard represents goals. You are probably competitive and you enjoy a challenge. It also suggests you are a highly creative, yet organised doodler.

Ball games

The ball doodle represents the interaction between two people, both sexually and otherwise. If the ball is shown in flight, then it shows that someone is throwing you the ball and asking you to run with it. You may have just been given an opportunity. The ball is in your court — you're being asked to show your

talents. It can represent challenges, competition, having and letting go, sexual play. It shows you are willing to make the most of life, never giving up and forever challenging yourself. Ball games also represent a longing to have a sense of belonging — either to a social group or team at work.

Line games

Doodles where you try and connect lines together in a certain, prescribed way, which are almost puzzle-like, represent the conflict you are trying to solve in your life. That conflict may be conscious and may be something to do with your relationships. More likely, however, is that you are striving unconsciously to resolve an imbalance between the functions of the psyche.

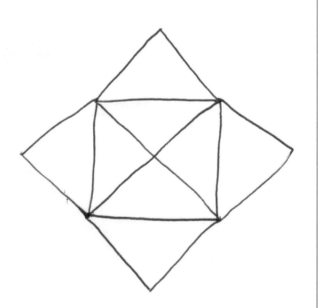

THE SCIENCE & PSYCHOLOGY OF

Gardens and landscapes

Gardens represent a search for tranquillity and serenity, as well as personal growth. You are essentially a romantic. Drawing a beautiful garden shows you are contented with your life. An overgrown garden represents that you know something needs to change. A square or circular garden shows you feel you have a bank of great wisdom which you need to access. The presence of a garden gate shows a need to defend yourself and those close to you. If the gate is closed it could mean that you are leaving something behind, signifying a change in your life.

Landscapes are a reflection of the nature loving part of your mind. It represents how you feel about yourself. A barren, arid landscape shows a pessimistic and despondent outlook. You need love and change in your life. A lush, fertile landscape symbolises a content, well balanced life with family and friends playing an important part.

Giraffe

The giraffe is a phallic symbol. You may have some sort of repressed anxiety about sex and your own sexuality. You could also have a fear of expressing your closely held emotions, which makes you difficult to get to know. If this is the case it is probably difficult to find someone who you feel comfortable enough with to open up to. You are likely to be quite witty and entertaining in an attempt to cover up what's really going on underneath.

Also see: Phallic symbols

Grape — see Food

Goat

The goat is an intensely sexual doodle showing you to be lustful and fertile. It is also an expression of your darker side. You are likely to be a very creative, diligent person. If your goat is tied up, however, you are expressing sadness or feelings of oppression within a sexual relationship.

On a lighter note, the goat can symbolise sure-footedness in life.

Gun — see Weapons

Hair

Doodles of hair are hugely symbolic and very sexual. Hair represents all sorts of things depending on the type of hair drawn. It can express your freedom, strength, individuality or lack of it. It can denote repression, celibacy and devotion.

Long hair represents a desire for spontaneous, free love. You are extremely adventurous sexually.

A bald or balding head shows sexual frustration and inhibition.

Spiky hair indicates that you are ordered but creative, and perhaps in need of some attention.

Curly hair shows you to be a romantic idealist who is exhausted with pressure and worry.

Tidy hair shows you to be disciplined and self-controlled. It can also show you to have a rather vain streak.

If you are male and you draw moustaches or beards, it can reflect an anxiety about sex and sexuality. It generally signifies low self-esteem and a desire to demonstrate virility.

A long beard indicates wisdom, serenity, old age and calm. When beards are doodled on women's faces, this could be a sign that you like to undermine women.

Also see: Face and Portrait

Hands and handcuffs

Hands show you to have a grasp of life and its surroundings. If you draw big hands, it shows you have a strong dominant personality, whereas small hands show a lack of confidence and social shyness. A lack of hands on the doodle of a whole figure shows sexual frustration. Dirty, shaded hands demonstrate social exclusion. Blood shown on hands shows insecurity or guilt.

Handcuffs symbolise anxiety and guilt. Also, you may be feeling overwhelmed by someone or by a situation, and you feel claustrophobic. Handcuffs can also represent sexual fantasy.

Hangman

If you draw a hangman it can represent guilt or a paranoia and fear of enemies. It also suggests that you are holding back your feelings, trying to kill emotions that you would rather suppress. Our emotions are generally expressed through sound such as laughing, crying, shouting etc. the hangman represents a desire to stifle these. You are likely to be feeling extremely frustrated and need sooner or later to share your problems.

Handbag – see Bag

Hare

The hare represents your strong creative impulses and intuition. You may seem fearful at first but once relaxed, you are dynamic, energetic and humourous. You are extremely flexible and can adapt easily and quickly in any number of environments.

The bigger the ears drawn on the hare, the more resourceful potential there is within you. If the hare features particularly sharp, big teeth then you may have an aggressive streak that rarely emerges except under extreme pressure.

Hat

The hat represents your beliefs and attitudes with regard to yourself and the world around you. A huge fancy hat implies a certain confidence and vanity, as well as a good dose of self-assurance. Large hats also reflect the importance of social position for you. You are very driven and ambitious in terms of financial success and admiration.

Other smaller hats indicate you are sensitive with a slightly defensive aspect in your personality. You are literally covering your head in an attempt to hide a part of the inner you. Thus, you may find it difficult sometimes to reveal what you are really thinking to others.

Hearts

The heart is the symbol of our very core, our essence. If you doodle hearts you are a deeply romantic person. A doodler who is deeply content and in love will draw hearts as will someone who is lovelorn or rejected.

The familiar drawing of a heart pierced with an arrow reveals a daydreaming, idealistic romantic. You will be determined to reconcile with your partner should matters go the wrong way. If you are single, you yearn for love. The shape of the point of the arrow is significant. The sharper the point, the more anger lurks in your unconscious. The rounder the point, the more content you feel in love. A heart with a rounded bottom shows a well balanced love indicating loyalty and fidelity to be your

priorities. A heart with an acute point indicates you to be a possessive, angry lover who places more importance on sex. A broken heart is generally a mirror of your own heart, portraying profound sadness perhaps due to a break up. A heart that has been shaded reveals that a great depression lurks within you that may or may not have come to the fore yet. A heart drawn within a circle demonstrates loneliness and sadness.

Overlapping hearts indicate that you are in a happy, well balanced relationship filled with love. Hearts within hearts reveal you to be a shy person who finds it difficult to communicate your innermost feelings to a partner leading possibly to feelings of frustration and jealousy.

Hedgehog

You are probably unconventional in your approach to life. You may feel anxious or slightly confused. The spikes of the hedgehog represent painful memories. Perhaps you are hurt or wounded emotionally and are feeling defensive, ready to lash out at someone.

Hill — see Mountain

Hippo

The hippo could indicate an anxiety about personal appearance and weight gain. It may also be evidence of a desire to slow down and take stock of your surroundings.

Horse

The horse is often depicted in mythology and folklore. As an animal it represents the non-human psyche — our animal side. It indicates the lower part of the body and the animal impulses that rise from there. This doodle reveals your dynamic, energetic side. You are subject to panics like all instinctive creatures. You probably feel you are visionary and powerful.

ANALYSING YOUR DOODLES

| *British author Jilly Cooper, known for her populist romances, draws a symbol of sexuality* | *British actress Lynn Redgrave doodles a horse revealing dynamism and energy* |

Horse — Winged

In Greek mythology, Pegasus was the winged horse who sprang from the blood of Medusa when Perseus cut off her head. It also refers to a large northern constellation of stars. If you doodle a winged horse, you may be interested in astronomy. You tend to be a daydreamer, and you feel the movements of the planets govern your life. You tend to listen to your heart and not your head, 'feeling' rather than 'thinking'.

Houses/buildings

The condition and structure of the houses/ buildings drawn are reflective of your mindset.

For example, a tumble down house reveals anxiety, trauma and a fear of ageing, but a strong castle shows a confidence and optimism that is often created by the establishment of a secure foundation in real life. If you often draw houses, you are prepared to build these foundations not only at home but also at work and with your family and friends.

The details within each doodle are significant also. A house with no doors or windows shows isolation, and an unwillingness

to be helped or approached.

When windows are plentiful, communication and involvement in the world are prevalent, as is social interaction.

Houses with gardens and fences demonstrate the importance you place on the sanctity of home and the security it represents.

If the house is under construction, it shows your willingness to repair past psychological trauma.

Buildings tend to be self-representing. Drawing a hospital, for example, shows a need and acceptance for healing.

Churches or temples show a deep craving for spirituality, or a cry for protection.

ANALYSING YOUR DOODLES

Footballer Frank Lampard doodles a house, which represents the sanctity of the home

Presenter Carol Smilie, appearing on home DIY TV shows, reveals the nature of her job

Human figures

The representation of human figures can reflect how you feel about yourself both physically and socially. There are many ways of drawing and grouping the human form. People drawn in groups tend to mean you are sociable and feel involved in the world. People drawn in couples could represent an unconscious feeling towards or relationship with your parents or partner.

People formed of geometric shapes such as cubes or triangles show you have a desire for structure in your life, which may be construed as detachment from others. It is likely that you are driven more by work than

intimate relationships.

Stick figures (matchstick men) show you to be a very driven individual who is extremely intelligent and decisive but who may fail in a social context. More realistic representations of people are equally important.

Childlike representations reflect a need for guidance and innocence. Giants can often symbolise fearful relationships with father figures and an urge to rebel. Figures drawn with extremely large shoulders or big muscles show a desire for authority and dominance based on insecurities — emotionally, socially and physically. Doodles of small people show an unconscious need for personal development and emotional interaction. Round people tend to be doodled if you are content and

humourous. Nude drawings reveal you to have strong sexual urges. You may feel oppressed sexually and long to rebel against society's norms. Nudes can also demonstrate a longing for somebody who is unavailable, or may also represent a need to make something known, to reveal a part of your character.

Snooker player Steve Davis draws a matchstick man holding a cue

Actor Sir Roger Moore, of James Bond fame alludes to his 'Saint' days

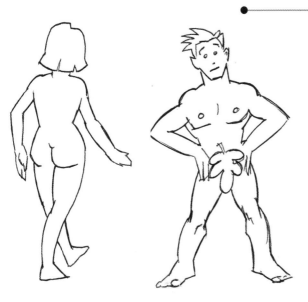

Insects and spiders

Insects tend to demonstrate a disdain for intimacy and sex, and a feeling of a lack of power and insignificance (among the swarm). Cockroaches, beetles and spiders show these insecurities the most strongly. It is likely that you try to cover up these weaknesses through hard work.

Spiders, especially when in webs, reveal a fear of domination perhaps stemming from a strong maternal influence, or a feeling of entrapment. Beetles, ants and cockroaches all express a deep self-loathing and you will probably fear sex or see it as something dirty.

Scorpions and wasps are not sexually motivated. These come from paranoid

thoughts and a fear of betrayal. However, you are ready to sting back in self-defence.

Ladybirds, butterflies and caterpillars mean you are at peace with yourself, yet always searching for balance and harmony in personal and professional contexts. An unwillingness to be restricted means there could be frequent changes in your life but all in the name of striving for perfection. Ladybirds are the most sensitive representations of these three.

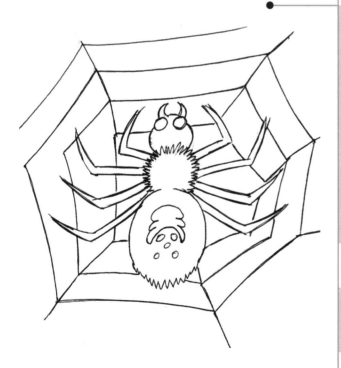

Also see: Ant, Bee, Beetle and Caterpillar

Insertion doodles

Insertion i.e. any object which goes inside another, such as keys in keyholes, plugs in sockets etc. demonstrate strong sexual desire that is unfulfilled. If you doodle this you may need some kind of outlet such as sporting or physical activities. It could also represent other unsolvable frustrations and a sense of entrapment and the need for escape.

I just love being alone. 6.8.04

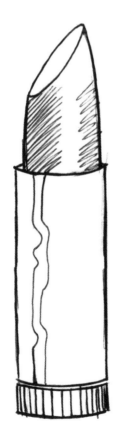

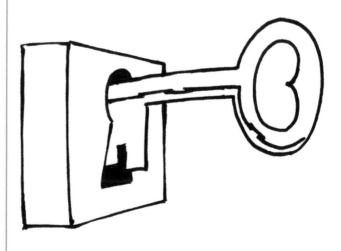

Also see: Cigarette/Cigar and Key

Island

Doodling islands is a poignant expression of loneliness and isolation. The depiction of a desert island often with a palm tree in the middle reveals an urgent need to escape the daily grind and discover a new stress-free lifestyle. You probably have a vivid imagination and escapist tendencies.

An island with a tree on it shows a desire to increase financial and emotional stability. You may also be someone who doesn't make friends very easily, but you value family and long term partnerships.

Jewellery

Drawing jewellery implies material lust and ambition. You may also have a tendency to show off. Necklaces reflect social status but also feelings of constraint and restriction. Bracelets and rings are very interesting as in their circular form they represent eternity and the world. Jung described the soul as being round. These doodles represent the most harmonious aspects of life: balance, contentment, and infinity. You are probably well balanced and prefer happy long-term monogamous relationships. Rings are an ancient symbol of commitment and the same applies to rings that are doodled. The ring may also reveal a strong wish for commitment that has yet to be fulfiled.

Also see: Earrings

ANALYSING YOUR DOODLES

Key

The key is an ancient symbol of wisdom. It also represents freedom and the wish to start afresh and open a new chapter of your life. Keys are also solutions to things that have been closed often for considerable lengths of time. Two questions can be asked in this case. Is the key symbolic of opening yourself up? Or is it the unlocking of somebody else's inner self perhaps a romantic prospect?

A shaded key could represent something that has been repressed, locked away and hidden perhaps to the detriment of the doodler.

Kite

The kite reflects a need for escape and a desire for change. You may be feeling claustrophobic, hemmed in. You tend to be extremely creative and imaginative, thus finding it difficult to be restricted in any way. The freedom that is associated with you is linked to wealth: cultural or material.

The positioning of the kite string in relation to the ground is important when interpreting this doodle. The closer the kite string is to the ground, the more achievable your goal in life. The kite string that trails through the sky implies dreams that may not be realised.

Knot

To doodle a knot implies some kind of confusion or tangle often within close familial relationships. It could represent frustration with the ties you have with your parents, and particularly mothers as the knot can represent the umbilical cord. There is an element of something unfinished about this doodle, of issues that need to be addressed.

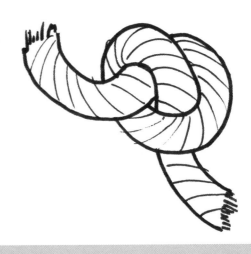

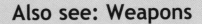

Knife

To doodle a knife is an expression of anger and paranoia, perhaps in response to some kind of defeat. A sharp knife denotes that you fear an encroaching enemy. Also seen as a phallic symbol, it can represent sexuality. It can also be interpreted as a need to cut yourself free of something or someone in your life.

Also see: Weapons

Lizard

The lizard symbolises a detachment from the world that is not self-imposed. The world feels cold and hard for you. There is an implication of suppression and denial of certain darker elements within your personality. Lizards lack malice and perhaps your adaptive skills are used to melt into the background like a chameleon.

Ladder

Drawing ladders reveals your aspirations. A strong, sturdy ladder implies a confidence and determination in material matters, as well as assertive performance in the workplace. To draw a broken ladder reveals a deep insecurity and uncertainty as to what the future holds. The ladder also represents an escape and risk taking.

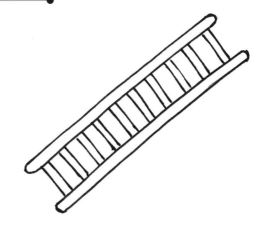

Lamb

This is a deeply symbolic doodle, which represents innocence and childhood. It displays a vulnerability and longing for purity. It is also an extremely powerful symbol of inner strength with biblical allusions. Are you self-sacrificing? Maybe your lack of selfishness needs to be recognised by others.

Leaves

Leaves represent the living growing aspects of people and reveal a deep love of nature. The shape of the leaves says more about you. To draw leaves with pointed tips, e.g. holly, shows your tough, spiky personality that does not suffer fools gladly, but is not prepared to accept criticism. Round leaves show a content, happy person with a great sense of humour and vivid imagination. Clover shows confidence and fertility. (Also see clover)

Leopard

Certain elements of anger, courage and passion are implied in this doodle. The passion could be directed towards protection and defence of children. It also signals the presence of your sexual urges. You may be looking for the perfect mate, aware that your biological clock is kicking.

The leopard's spots can be interpreted as eyes, meaning an awareness and watchfulness of the world.

Also see: Animals

Lion

Doodling lions implies an inner strength, resolve and huge appetite for life. You are lustful in terms of control and power. You have excellent social skills. You achieve your goals and command a huge amount of respect as a consequence. However, there is a strong self-destructive streak that you are aware of and fear. Your strong sexual drive can also be extremely self-destructive and another cause for concern.

Historically, lions have always been symbolic of strength and loyalty and these are qualities that you possess in abundance. Lions are fierce defenders of what they believe to be true and of whom they love. The female doodler of lions would probably have a strong, dominant personality perhaps with a complex paternal relationship.

Lips

Lips are very sexual, and can also be interpreted as mimicking female genitalia. A confident sexual lover draws full lips. Thin lips show a lack of sensuality and meanness in personal relations. Small lips imply discretion. Parted lips reveal someone who is actively searching for a new relationship and is an adept flirt.

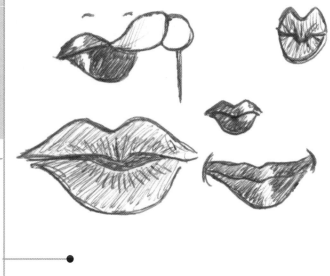

Singer Patti Boulaye draws lips, representing the tool she uses in her singing profession

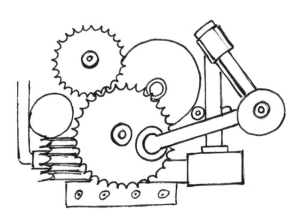

Machine

To doodle a machine relates directly to the body. Drawing an engine, for example, refers to the heart. The more complicated the machine, the more likely it is representing the brain. Drawing machines can also show an acceptance of the lack of control over the body in terms of ageing and illness.

Map and compass

You are attempting to find a direction you feel confident and secure about. At the moment there is doubt about where your life is heading.

Drawing a map and compass reveals a search for direction either in work or love. The act of drawing a map implies a willingness to be active in the search.

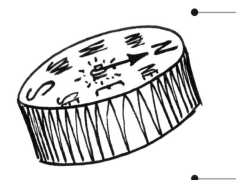

Mask

A mask implies a shyness and strong need for privacy. Thus the mask represents a facade, something for the outside world to see that is not reflective of what goes on in your inner world.

Conversely, the mask doodle can also show you have a strong urge to finally reveal yourself, and share who you really are with others.

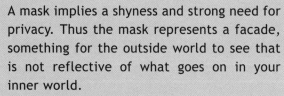

Also see: Faces and Portraits

Maze

A maze shows a confusion and need for guidance through difficult choices that have to be made in life. The fear of becoming lost in life is very strong here and the maze could be an attempt to rationalise conscious thought to enable decision-making. These doodles can also be interpreted as a request for help from others for direction. You may feel overwhelmed by the infinite number of choices. More intricate labyrinthine doodles represent the same thing but at a much more intense and anxious level. Your thoughts and decisions are more complex, and consequently you feel more confused.

Medicine

Doodling medicines such as ointments and pills reveal an unconscious anxiety about your health. Depending on the frequency of these drawings, you may well be a hypochondriac. Or it may represent the need to be healed or made better perhaps in a close relationship. This is a positive remedial unconscious thought.

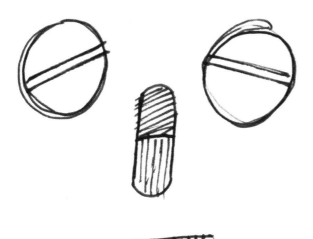

Also see: Shapes and Circles

Money

Money represents value — our own self-worth and what we have materially. It also represents power. To doodle money as actual representations of money, i.e. notes and coins, represents a deep-rooted insecurity coupled with a powerful drive to make money to compensate for this. The drive to make money could mean your partner is often neglected because of your inability to express yourself verbally. The emphasis you place on financial and material things is an unconscious attempt to cover up your true emotions. Drawing symbols, i.e. pound or dollar signs, also shows a desire for wealth and material gain. You may be feeling dissatisfaction with your current financial situation.

Monkey — see Ape

Monsters

Drawing monsters is essentially drawing the darker, unknown parts of the self with an underlying fear of this darker side. Approaching yourself tentatively but with an open, accepting mind could allay these fears. The other dark aspect of this doodle is a self-reference to some kind of act or deed committed. The more spiky or detailed, i.e. fangs and claws, the more deep-rooted the guilt or fear of the darker elements of yourself. Perhaps there is some self-loathing involved.

Also see: Dragons

Moon

The moon is a romantic symbol that is predominantly feminine with its relationship to the menstrual cycle. There is an element of renewal and the eternal cycle of life. Doodles of the moon show you to be deeply dreamy and full of romantic notions. Passion is also prevalent and a strong desire for the unattainable. Moons drawn at different stages of the lunar cycle mean different things. A crescent moon implies some kind of wish for change; facing right it implies a desire for your aspirations to be realised in the future. Underlying all this is something mysterious, an inexplicable attraction etc. The moon is also closely linked to the tides and madness. As a complete circle, it is associated with wholeness and represents the soul.

Mouse

The mouse represents small fears and irritations encountered in daily life. There is an underlying anxiety here or perhaps you are particularly self-conscious, even painfully shy. You may have a sense of being slowly worn down and in need of a change. Depictions of cartoon mice reveal your deeply immature side. You are constantly in need of some kind of reassurance because of your deep-rooted insecurity.

Also see: Animals and Rat

Mountains

Mountains are spiritual doodles. They signify the struggle you face within yourself and the hurdles you overcome in life. They can also symbolise something momentous that has happened or is about to happen. There is an element of isolation in these doodles that stems from the personal journey within you. There are many ways to doodle mountains, each representing something different. A smooth mountain implies somebody who works steadily and methodically, managing to achieve targets. Rugged mountains demonstrate a person with absolute conviction who will fight any obstacle. A doodle showing a figure standing at the top indicates somebody who craves some insight into the mysteries of life. A dark, shaded mountain shows a depression or low time in your life.

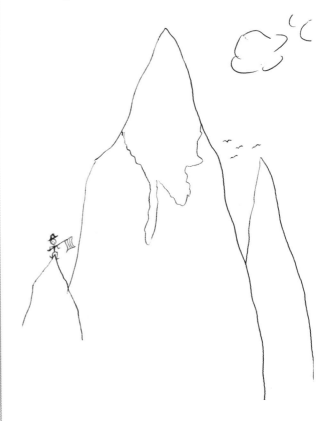

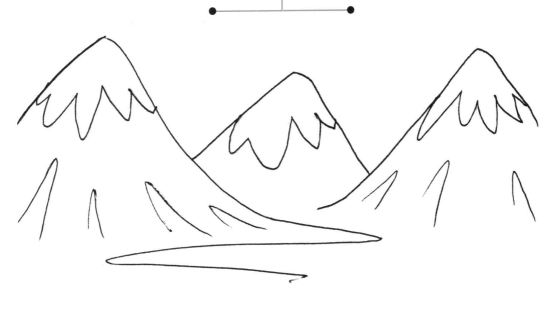

Musical Instruments

Different musical instruments represent different aspects of the emotional self with a strong sexual undercurrent physically. Practically all musical instruments symbolise the sexual organs. Organs represent solidity in friendships and love. Pianos show a harmonious sexual relationship that is tender and respectful. Guitars are the most commonly doodled. They show you are quite good at seduction. Flutes symbolise happiness and sociability. A harp, particularly if it is broken, means sadness and heartbreak. The drums represent a period of transition, as do all percussion instruments.

Musical instruments demonstrate creativity and humour, as well as confidence and clarity of expression.

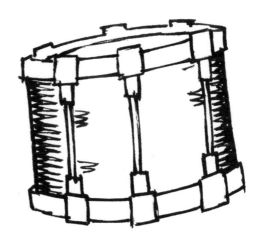

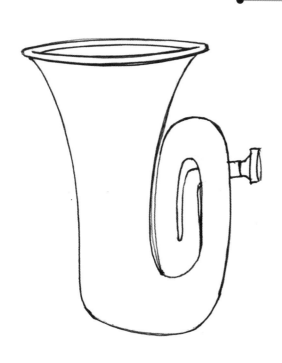

Names and signatures

Names are essentially representative of yourself and your identity. There is an undertone of egomania if you write your name repeatedly and a need for reassurance and affirmation. A desire for attention is also evident.

If you write your name in large letters, you probably have a larger than life personality and you are a good entertainer. If you write your name in very small letters it shows a certain lack of confidence. To write somebody else's name repeatedly shows an obsessive personality.

To draw a circle around someone's name is a defensive action. To draw a circle around your own name indicates a lack of trust and feeling of isolation. Signatures that have a line underneath signify self-importance.

July 2001

Jeffrey Archer

July 2003

Jeffrey Archer

Novelist Jeffrey Archer doodles his name with expressive faces

British actor Jeremy Irons' doodle of his name with a few decorative frills

Nest

A nest generally represents home and an emotional dependence on parents/carers. You may have a strong desire to build a home and start a family. You are probably very committed and monogamous, but you need this security for absolute contentment. Depictions of broken or unfinished nests reveal you to have a lack of commitment and you feel constrained in your domestic situation. Nest drawing is very feminine.

Numbers

Numbers often have a lot of personal significance — age, numbers of houses, dates, passage of time and telephone numbers. Often doodling numbers reveals an organised mathematical, even scientific mind. Usually doodlers will repeat the same number continuously.

0: The eternal circle, nothingness, the void, space, everything, unity, wholeness.
1: A beginning. Indicates the desire for newfound independence. Can show egocentric tendencies.
2: Balance, duality, relationships, opposites

and conflict.
3: The triangle, creativity and reproduction. (A need to get through something problematic.)
4: Represents the elements — earth, air, fire, and water. Signifies harmony and balance. Also infers that you are a good organiser.
5: Humanity — the number of digits on each limb and the five senses. Sometimes interpreted as a fascination and drive to accumulate money but also a desire to escape from the past and move forward.
6: Symmetry, the unity of mind and body. Also symbolises sex and a materialistic streak.
7: Cyclic, number of days in the week, number of musical notes symbolising wholeness. Could reveal anxiety about ageing.
8: Infinity, death and resurrection. Shows a

strong urge for personal development.

9: Associated with unity of male and female, and hence childbirth.

10: Denotes idealism and perfection; the start of a new beginning; optimism.

11: Symbolises something coming to an end.

12: A full cycle; 12 months a year; 12 hour clocks; 12 disciples.

Sometimes people write random long series of numbers while displaying mathematical skill. These numbers display a lot of self-absorption; and these series are designed to impress. Repeated writing of the numbers 666 implies a fascination or obsession with the occult. Some people believe this to be the sign of the devil.

Oasis

The oasis has a very similar interpretation to an island. You have a deep sense of loneliness even though you may be in a relationship. You are unable to trust people and are unlikely to feel secure in your relationships.

The trees (usually palm trees) that are drawn in these doodles reveal a desire to escape and be free. While this escapist tendency is going to help in the short run, you will need to face up to your problems sooner or later. The roots of your woes may rest in the relationship you have or had with your mother or father.

Also see: Island and Trees

Octopus

Doodling an octopus shows a very strong attachment to the mother (figure) but also shows a strong desire for independence and a chance to discover your individuality rather than be part of a unit. The tentacles can also represent a wish to entangle or entrap somebody who is trying to stand back or withdraw from a partnership/relationship. In extreme cases the tentacles could be an unconscious desire to consume the escapee completely before they escape. You may find yourself having to cling onto things, stopping them from slipping away. You are constantly juggling your work and personal life. This may mean that work and partners get neglected.

Pan, pot

If you draw pots and pans you are comfortable and open with yourself and others. This extends to your sexual relationships. This doodle is essentially feminine and implies a lot of creativity — in the field of cooking or 3-D arts and crafts, ceramics, sculpture etc. There is also an element of providing and taking care of others in a maternal sense. You are always hospitable and generous. Your caring and giving side is born from the strong bond you have or had with your mother. You are a good listener and this does not go unnoticed by your friends who often seek your advice on personal matters.

ANALYSING YOUR DOODLES

Parachute

If you doodle parachutes you may be feeling constrained and long for some kind of escape. Unfortunately there is a massive fear of the unknown that is why the figure has a parachute, as a safety device rather than free falling.

This doodle could also represent a recent difficult escape from personal situations or an unconscious desire that some kind of escape is necessary and looming. There is a dreamy element to your personality. You may be trying to find a way to get back down to earth. There could also be some anxiety issues concerning failure (falling).

Plant

You would generally doodle plants if you have a strong and loving relationship with nature. The density of the foliage doodled reflects levels of control you have over your life. To draw wilting or dead plants, as Van Gogh often did, shows an underlying sadness probably due to some kind of loss or even exhaustion. You have a need to step back and revitalise.

To draw weeds implies a lack of control and need for personal strength and growth. As with leaves the spikier the detail the more anger and aggression lies within. The rounder the detail, the more content and relaxed you are.

Phallic symbols

Men generally draw these. These symbols range from aeroplanes, animal horns, buildings including lighthouses, skyscrapers, church steeples, towers, pens, pencils, missiles, rockets, spears, pipes — even some vegetables can be described as phallic — carrots, leeks, turnips, cucumbers etc. All these symbols represent a lack of sexual activity and sexual drive. You have probably been attempting to relieve these frustrations through doodling and fantasy. If the symbol has a broken or crumpled appearance this could represent a fear of sexual failure, impotence, premature ejaculation, not satisfying a partner. Women do doodle phallic symbols but these are generally humourous. (Also see: Rocket)

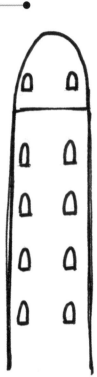

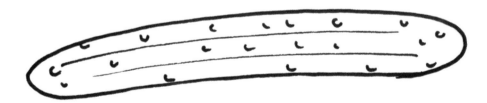

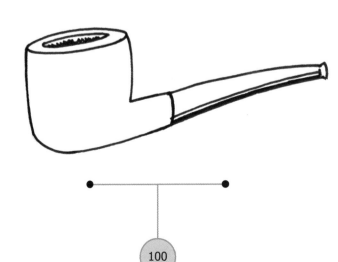

Pig

Drawing a pig may symbolise a latent fertility but generally leans towards an anxiety and self-consciousness about appearance, particularly weight and general body shape.

This doodle also reveals a certain amount of uncontrollable desire and appetite. You are likely to be very sensual. Although you may become disillusioned with your lack of discipline at times, you nevertheless retain a cheeky sense of humour.

Piano — see Musical Inst.

Actress Betty Driver, soap star of UK TV's Coronation Street, doodles a pig

British politician Clare Short also doodles a cute, round pig

Portraits/self-portrait

Portraits are generally drawn by adolescents striving for a sense of identity. In later years, the self-portrait shows that you have firmly impressed your own identity on others and made your mark in the world. Drawn in profile they can represent an introverted personality, however, the self-portrait would normally reveal an extravert. Your energies flow outwards, and you are more concerned with doing rather than thinking. You are a sentimentalist and your emotions, more than your head, motivate you in decision-making. Such doodles tend to be drawn by actors, teachers, politicians, musicians, comedians, authors, playwrights etc. — professions which involve revealing yourself to an audience. Comical faces tend to be drawn by men, and points to their need to be the centre of attention.

Elton John, musician

Also see: Faces

Brain Blessed, actor

Ron Moody, actor

ANALYSING YOUR DOODLES

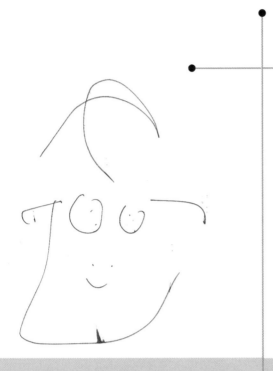

Alan Bennett, playwright

Phil Collins, musician

Richard E Grant, actor

Twiggy, actress and former Sixties' model

Presents and parcels

These doodles indicate that something needs to be revealed, which has been concealed for a long time. It may also symbolise that your feelings have been kept wrapped up and tidied away into a box i.e. compartmentalised. There is a strong feeling of anticipation within this drawing and a need to open up.

The more ornate the packaging and detail of the present, the deeper the emotions contained within. There could also be an element of insecurity and a need to be accepted amongst peers by perhaps quite literally presenting yourself as you truly are.

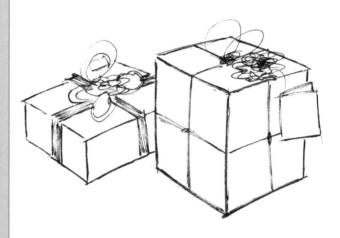

Queen

Drawing a queen represents a maternal figure or influence that you are thinking about. There is an implication that this figure is remote or distant and therefore the queen represents a need for acknowledgment of the relationship. There is a strong possibility that it is also evidence of a newfound confidence that needs some kind of recognition.

The addition of a crown to this doodle reveals egocentric tendencies. You ooze self-confidence, and you can be fairly materialistic. You are also domineering and authoritative. You feel that you have the whole world eating out of the palm of your hand.

ANALYSING YOUR DOODLES

Question marks

This is a common doodle with multi-faceted meanings. When you are in a situation in which you are presented with a number of choices, and you doodle question marks, it symbolises complex dilemmas and a state of indecision.

You display a strong sense of rationality, but may become forceful when needing information. There is a distinct lack of resolution and a fear of making the wrong decision.

Alternatively, it can reveal an inquisitive mind, which never accepts a truth but always challenges it.

Rabbit

This could represent a yearning for children and is a traditional symbol of fertility and spirituality. Rabbits also symbolise rampant sexuality, but sexuality with a view to procreation rather than carnal pleasure. The image of the rabbit as a soft, non-threatening creature is a reflection of your personality. Unfortunately, it may mean that you can be taken advantage of and feel threatened by more predatory characters. You tend to be home loving and once settled you like to hide away within your own secure world.

Also see: Hare

Rainbow

A daydreamer would most likely doodle a rainbow. The rainbow is a symbol of hope and understanding. You are in harmony with nature and the seasons. There is a calm acceptance of the world as it is and you have an optimistic outlook.

You tend to have simple, enduring and monogamous relationships and you are attracted to the more spiritual side of life. You may be a person who loves colour: your home is likely to be filled with colour and beautiful things.

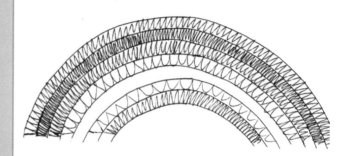

Also see: Shapes and swirls

Rain drops

Like tear drops, rain can be a sign of depression. You may be going through a bad patch and are unlikely to be able to see much apart from gloom and doom ahead of you.

Alternatively, rain is a symbol of vitality and necessary for growth and life. It suggests a need for nourishment, maybe your own nourishment, or else a wish for growth of some sort.

Also see: Tear drops and Clouds

Ram

This is an extremely masculine symbol. The ram is a potent historical symbol that features in the Bible and the Koran. You probably see yourself as a dominant member of a group, even the leader. The horns are very phallic so the drawing could also allude to some kind of sexual frustration or need for sexual dominance. The shape and size of the horns is indicative of your determination in romantic pursuits. The larger and sharper the horns, the more ruthless you will be. Another strong symbolic aspect of the ram is fertility. If you are a female, you have the potential to be sexually demanding.

Rat

You may have a deep sense of self-loathing, maybe as a result of a recent action. You are probably feeling quite guilty about whether you are responsible or not. It can be quite a negative symbol with an underlying motivation. It may also reveal a repression of particular characteristics within yourself that you are uncomfortable with. Details such as an extremely long tail reveal how deeply these issues lie: the longer the tail, the deeper the guilt or issue. You may feel discomfort about the darker more furtive aspects of your personality. You may also have a gnawing fear of getting older.

Religious symbols

The concept of the self is of paramount importance in psychology, but is opposite in meaning when it comes to theology. In psychology the religious figures point to the self, whereas in theology the self points to a central figure. Thus, in theology the psychological self is an allegory of Christ. The Christ-symbol is, therefore, of great significance. It is perhaps the most developed and differentiated symbol of the self, apart from the figure of the Buddha.

To doodle any religious symbol, be it a cross, Buddha, Christ, fish etc. it shows your spiritual quest and your journey to self-awareness and spiritual enlightenment.

my beautiful Buddha's head

Joanna Lumley

British actress Joanna Lumley doodles a Buddha's head, a significant religious symbol

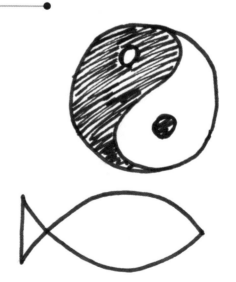

River

A river symbolises emotions, sexuality and powerful forces of change and even despair (drowning). To draw a wide, flowing river means a strong sexual desire and fecund personality. To draw a bridge across the river symbolises a transition.

If someone is featured in the water this could show a feeling of being overwhelmed by life. A floating person reveals that you have a confident and relaxed attitude. A rushing river shows you have huge amounts of energy that perhaps needs a very specific focus and direction. A long twisting river relates to the twists and turns in life. Drawing rivers can also demonstrate a strong sense of humour.

Ring — see Jewellery

Road

Doodles of roads have similar connotations as rivers, but also a much stronger and definite direction is implied. Crossroads indicate major decisions and uncertainty about what to do in your life. A road that comes to a dead end indicates frustration and a need for change. You may be feeling claustrophobic and your life smacks of stagnancy. A motorway demonstrates a need to find a quick solution to a dilemma. To doodle a fork in the road implies a parting of ways. A track leading off the road means quite literally being sidetracked or distracted. A road going ahead shows an openness to uncertainty about the future and a confident outlook.

Robot

A doodle of a robot reveals a need for change and the feeling of being stuck in a rut. The more complex the structure of the robot, the more complicated the situation is to fix. The person may also feel as though they are socially repressed and incapable of fluid natural responses in social situations. This could reflect an anxiety about the future. There is an underlying defensive atmosphere surrounding these kinds of doodles. The metal structure acts as a protective shield, mimicking your own defences and shows a need to protect yourself from outside forces. You probably tend to listen to your head, more than your heart. You would most likely have a practical, logical mind.

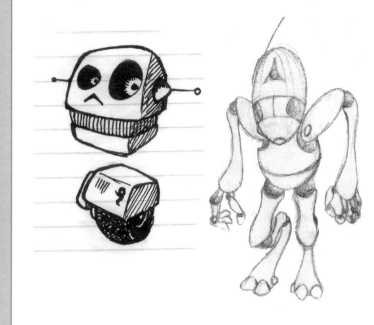

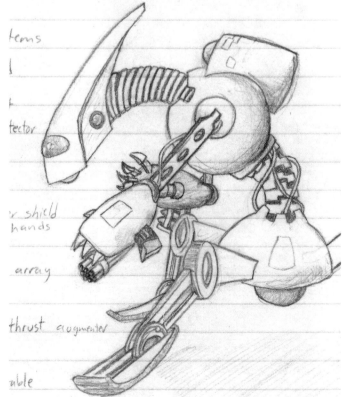

Rocket

This is an extremely phallic drawing that reveals a strong sense of professional ambition. There could be some kind of sexual anxiety present — maybe a threat from another male, leading to sexual frustration.

However, huge flames flowing from the base of the rocket could signify a lack of thrust and direction in your life. You may literally need a rocket to get you back into gear again.

It is likely that the field of science is of interest to you. Your thirst for adventure is evident and if you manage to fuel your own fantasies the sky is the limit for you. Rockets are more commonly drawn by men.

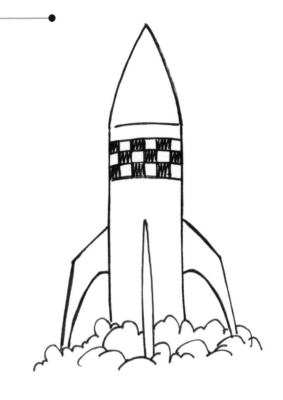

Roller coaster

These doodles may indicate that you have a problematic sexual life and a complex personal life. You may be extremely happy at one instance and suddenly become very depressed very quickly.

Your emotional life is 'up and down', stemming from the phrase 'emotional roller coaster'. You may have a deep insecurity that needs to be addressed. This insecurity is probably deeply-rooted in your unconscious and it may take quite a journey of self discovery in order to find out why it is there. Where there is self-doubt, there is a reason behind it. Listen to the warning signs.

THE SCIENCE & PSYCHOLOGY OF

Rose

To draw a rose reveals a sensitive, romantic nature. You are fundamentally an idealist. Roses can also symbolise female sexual organs and are essentially very feminine doodles. Roses that feature sharp thorns show an awareness of suffering. There may be an underlying sense of aggression stemming from episodes in which you have suffered greatly. You pay attention to detail and always strive for perfection.

Sea

The sea symbolises life, the deepest parts of the unconscious and the boundaries with the conscious mind. The sea is a powerful symbol and represents the drive for life and the goals you wish to achieve such as independence and procreation. It also symbolises energy. A calm sea indicates contentment and serenity. A choppy sea reveals anxiety and urgency, as well as a strong desire to settle down.

A figure in the sea indicates a sense of being overwhelmed and fear of going under. The sea is also associated with the mother figure. If waves are a feature of the drawing, they can indicate some kind of anxiety, probably sexually. Seaweed featured could be associated with a fear of being dragged down by something or someone in your life.

ANALYSING YOUR DOODLES

Scales

These are traditionally a symbol of justice. There could be a feeling of injustice or lack of balance present in your life. Scales also reveal your strong intellectual side. You are also quite cautious and patient. Scales that are heavily weighted to one side show anxiety and inability to make a decision.

As in all of us there tends to be something in our psyche that is out of balance, Jung believed that in ones journey to achieving 'personality', opposites in our psyche become unified. Drawing scales can represent your path to finding yourself and striving towards wholeness, equilibrium and peace.

Shark

A shark can represent the fear of a predatory person who is dominating you. You are literally being devoured by this person emotionally, so much so that the shark represents a fear of death. You are not sure how long you can emotionally stand the situation you are in. You may not even be conscious of this, but look around you — is there someone, perhaps an elder sibling, father or authority figure in your life who you feel is dominating you? If you don't pay attention and speak up, every now and then you run the risk of losing your own identity. The shark is telling you that you are scared to stand up for yourself.

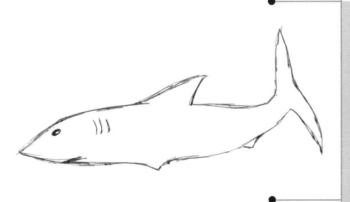

Shapes and swirls

These doodles are essentially abstract and the result of distracted minds. They can be very revealing. Practically everyone draws shapes and swirls at some point in their doodling.

Boxes and cubes
These are demonstrative of a practical person. You are likely to be extremely hard working and finish things properly. You are very methodical and efficient, with an element of cautiousness.

Pyramids
You may be attracted to the spiritual world and

the occult. Females who draw pyramids are fascinated with sex and all things feminine. A male who draws pyramids is sexually very unpredictable and lurches from warmth to extreme coldness when sexually satisfied.

Cylinders
You have a practical mind and calm nature.

Triangles
Upward-pointing triangles are essentially masculine and represent fire. You are probably inquisitive and seek answers to intellectual problems. You are prepared to take risks and you have a strong personality. Downward pointing triangles are representative of your feminine side and represent water. You are

calm and serene and lack ambition. You are mentally very perceptive and intellectually active. You have a sense of searching for answers. You can be quite harsh on yourself and are easily heart-broken.

Triangles with another triangle inside show that you may feel threatened. Your anger is a defensive measure.

Circles represent wholeness – see Circles

Squares

These reveal that you are solid and stable, as well as practical and constant. You have a strong need for security and stability in personal relationships. Squares drawn inside other squares reflect defensiveness. You may feel

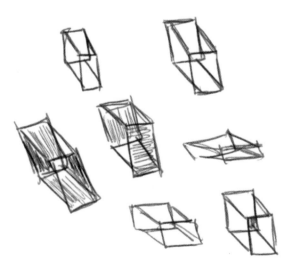

trapped and claustrophobic. A collection of squares may show some sort of frustration.

Diamonds and hexagons

Perfectly drawn, these show you to be an extremely efficient person who is driven by very specific goals.

Swirls and spirals

Swirls can reveal a lack of direction and restlessness within you. Spirals show that you tend to dwell on problems. You may appear withdrawn and can suffer from sexual repression. You possess a desperate need for security, and can be jealous and possessive. Spirals that start in the centre reveal a lot of tension and angst. If you draw spirals that start from the

outside and end in the centre, it reveals a desire for specific targets and finite situations.

Lines

A collection of horizontal lines reveals a good level of concentration and an ability to keep calm under pressure. Lines drawn diagonally reveal a strong need to dominate. If the lines have even spaces between them, it demonstrates a strong sense of balance, but you may have controlling tendencies in personal relationships.

Underlining any doodle, gives it prominence and importance. It can reveal an underlying tension and possibly arrogant tendencies.

Crosses

These represent an unknown quantity. There are also underlying religious tones. You may have a negative outlook and can be prone to self-destruction.

Loops

These can reveal a need to alleviate stress. The wider the loop, the greater your imagination and the more empathy you possess. Very narrow loops indicate some kind of repressed anxiety.

Zigzags

These show a lot of anger and pent up frustration. You do not respond well to being directed. You are hard working. The sharper the peaks of

the zigzags, the more aggression there is inside you. You have a need for comfort to alleviate your frustrations.

Arches
Drawn repetitively, these demonstrate a tough person who is incredibly loyal. You are intensely private and demonstrate high levels of self-control in social situations.

Upside-down arches
These reveal an individual with a strong sense of self who is extremely sociable. You have a need for acceptance and are often kind, helpful, generous and blessed with good humour. There is an openness and honesty about you, which makes you attractive.

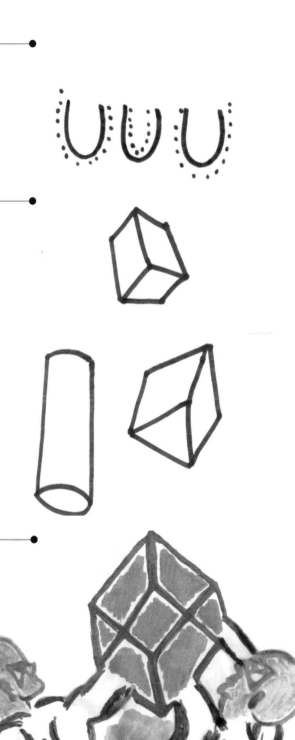

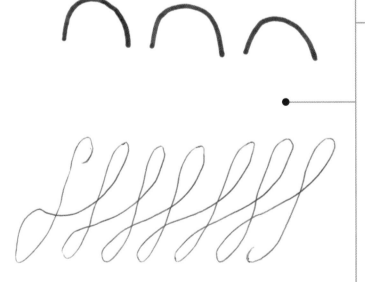

THE SCIENCE & PSYCHOLOGY OF

Shell

Seashells show that you love nature and have a huge respect and love of beauty. You demand honesty in all aspects of your life. You can find life in the fast lane difficult and can become withdrawn when things become overwhelming.

Shoes

These reveal an interest in personal appearance. The more ornate the shoe the more vain you are. They also represent an element of reflection in your social standing and emotional stability. High heel shoes are overtly sexual. You may have a high sex drive and be temporarily frustrated. The need to be desired is extremely important to you and as a result you can often be vulnerable. The more practical the shoe, the more practical you are. These doodles are most commonly drawn by women and could also imply some material lust.

Shoe designer Manolo Blahnik predictably doodles one of his beautiful creations

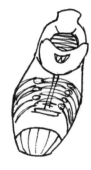

Ship — see Boat

Skeleton

Drawing skeletons reveals a desire for an issue to be stripped down and simplified, and can reveal a deep-seated fear of death, showing an unconscious realisation of your mortality. There may also be an element in your character that you have tried to kill off and this doodle could be an acknowledgement of that.

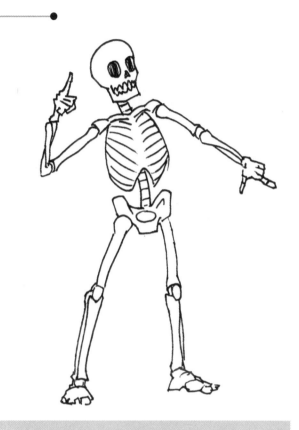

Skull

Drawing a skull means you are concentrating on the issue of death, but with a view to making more of your life. To draw some crossbones underneath the skull represents a need for change as you feel hemmed in and restless. You are probably strong willed and capable of taking chances and consequently will not be stuck in a rut for long.

Skeletons and skulls are obviously quite a morbid subject matter for a doodle and may reflect an interest in the occult, or you may have an interest in the spirit of adventure. Generally you like to live your life on the edge, no one could ever say you were boring.

Snail

You are very defensive by nature and tend to withdraw into your shell when you are stressed or upset. You may be quite insecure and as a result extremely cautious at work and socially. You become embarrassed easily especially when talk turns to matters sexual. The snail is drawn by women most commonly. The way the shell is drawn is another indicator of your psyche. See 'Spirals' in 'Shapes and Swirls'. The antennae could be regarded as phallic symbols depending on how erect they are. Floppy antennae point towards low self-esteem and depression. Erect antennae show a healthy regard for sexual matters.

Signature — see Name

Snake

Snakes and reptiles represent our most primitive urges and often indicate a need for power at the most basic of levels. Ancient symbolism is littered with images of serpents and snakes. The snake swallowing its own tail is the ancient symbol of infinity and a staff with a snake wrapped around it would only be wielded by a person of great arcane power. Snakes are usually, though not exclusively, drawn by men. When drawn by women, they may be a response to a sexual threat. Many cultures venerate snakes and serpents and imbue them with magical properties. Some cultures believe the snake to have powerful

aphrodisiac properties. They are one of the oldest religious symbols. In biblical terms the snake represents temptation as illustrated in the book of Genesis, which led to the destruction of the garden of Eden.

The snake doodled lengthways shows you are open, relaxed and sexually confident. This is phallic and implies both fertility and sexual prowess. Snakes drawn in a coil are a sign of insecurity and could even reveal some recent rebuff. A snake ready to strike, particularly a venomous one, shows aggression and sexual tension. This could either be from fear or base desire. Snakes drawn with open mouths and fangs betray you as a predatory person. Patterns drawn on the back of the snake indicate sexual or romantic feelings.

Snow

These doodles reveal your childlike, Peter Pan side. You long for the purity and innocence you had when you were young. There is also an underlying sense of nostalgia. You may feel quite lonely and isolated and therefore need some attention.

The responsibilities of adulthood are too much to manage and this is why you yearn for your childhood. You may be sexually repressed and find it difficult to achieve warm, close relationships. You can appear to be quite cold and distant but after an initial struggle you will eventually be able to relax. You also have a strong sense of aesthetics.

Spirit (the)

The spirit can take various forms. Most commonly it is in the form of a wise man or 'real' spirit such as a ghost. The wise old man can take the guise of an authority figure such as a doctor, priest, magician or teacher. It can also be, but more rarely, in the form of a gnome-like figure or a boy/youth. This could represent a situation in which you need insight and understanding, as well as determination and planning. It is also symbolic of a father-complex. In men this leads to an unwillingness to accept authority, but an ability to embrace spirituality. For women it also causes spiritual aspirations and interests.

Spaceship — see UFO

Stairs

Doodles of stairs represent your desire to take steps towards achieving something big. You are facing a challenge in your life and you know what you have to do to progress.

You are assertive and confident in your approach. You have strong leadership qualities and love challenges. Your drive and ambition are sure to get you where you want to be.

For men, going upstairs may represent erection and intercourse. For women, going downstairs may represent a sexual 'fall'.

Also see: Ladders

Stars

Stars are extremely common doodles and their shapes and design vary hugely. The star is a sign of hope and aspiration, and reflects your idealistic streak. You are likely to be extremely driven. A five-pointed star is associated with the elements — Fire, Water, Earth and Air. This symbol has been associated with witchcraft and could demonstrate an interest in the occult.

There could also be some need for balance in some aspects of a personal relationship, as well as a desire for harmony. You may be a very possessive lover.

To draw six-pointed stars (the star of

Sarah Ferguson, Duchess of York, doodles a six-pointed star

Solomon) shows balance and the importance of it i.e. the balance between the masculine and the feminine sides of the human psyche.

The upward triangle symbolises the masculine and downward the feminine.

To draw a star on top of something shows huge ambition and determination.

Drawing stars also demonstrates an awareness of the cosmos and being a part of it. You are also probably possessed with good social skills.

Also see: Shapes and swirls

Submarine

The submarine is a predominantly masculine doodle that has phallic implications. You may have some kind of sexual inhibition that has been kept well concealed in the depths of your unconscious. You may not feel confident in self-examination and suppress certain darker aspects of yourself. If any windows are detailed these imply that you have become aware of this and you are prepared to do something about it. Boats and submarines refer to relationships — perhaps you find it difficult to share your experiences with family friends and partners. If the submarine is shaded you may be feeling threatened and as a consequence become withdrawn.

Model Claudia Schiffer doodles a wind surfer flying towards the sun

Sun

The sun reflects your happiness, warmth and creativity. It is an optimistic life-affirming symbol that also represents fertility. The sun has been worshiped by many different cultures as diverse as the Mayans and ancient Egyptians who both had sun gods that were central to their religious practices. It is a common doodle drawn universally by adults and children alike, this means that these doodles are very revealing and offer lots of opportunities for analysis.

If you draw a sun unobscured by clouds, you are happy and full of hope for the future. You have a trusting nature, are full of confidence, extremely social and humourous. A doodle of the sun rising is an unconscious acknowledgement that a period of sadness is coming to an end, a fresh start is under way

and something new and optimistic is about to begin. You are sensitive and creative. A picture of the sun setting is a picture tinged with sadness and could be an unconscious anxiety of the ageing process, as well as an awareness of mortality. It could also be an unconscious acknowledgement of a close personal relationship that has come to an end.

A sun that appears to be hot, perhaps with flames sketched around the circumference, shows some simmering tensions that you are unable to express. You could become extremely angry and explode when the pressure becomes too much. Any drawing of the sun that is shaded reveals sadness and depression. The darker the shading, the deeper the sadness.

Doodles of the sun hidden behind clouds or mountains reveal a looming depression pertaining to an upset with close partners or

friends. You may find it a struggle to recover emotionally and become withdrawn as a way of coping. The sun reflected in water reveals a contemplative nature. You need to take time to consider your next move.

Pictures of the sun often feature faces and these reflect your state of mind. A smiling face indicates you are a happy, well balanced individual who anticipates the future readily and with confidence. Unhappy faces reveal an underlying sadness that may be being suppressed. You are concealing your sadness within the ostensibly upbeat, positive associations of the sun. To feature a hat on the sun means you are extremely confident and can occasionally be rather self-important.

THE SCIENCE & PSYCHOLOGY OF

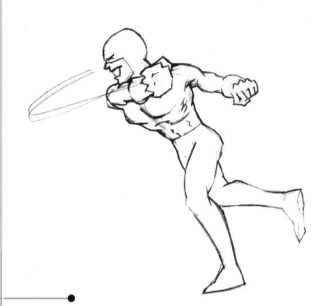

Superheroes

These doodles reveal feelings of inadequacy and self-doubt. You are expressing an idealised version of yourself which you secretly desire. These fantasy doodles partly reflect the role you wish to play in real life but may not be able to. Heroic figures show a desire to metamorphosise and can also reflect passage of time and personal growth, for example the transition from adolescence to adulthood.

British presenter and film buff Jonathan Ross doodles the superhero spiderman

ANALYSING YOUR DOODLES

Table

These doodles are evidence of your practical side. You are probably extremely hard working and approach tasks methodically. There is an element of domesticity present, as well as good social skills. You have a steady, fulfiling social life which is very important to you. You tend to be reliable and stable.

Tear drops

These are a reflection of your emotional suffering. You are currently feeling fragile and vulnerable. You are extremely sensitive and require a lot of love and kindness. You may feel unable to communicate verbally. Your sadness and need for some kind of release is expressed by drawing tear drops. Have a good cry, it may help. This is essentially a feminine doodle.

Teddy bear

You are very demonstrative in your affections and emotionally dependent. The teddy bear can represent a need for some kind of parental substitute. This may be an expression of a desire for sympathy from others. In relationships you require love, but don't necessarily need passion. You may have a slightly naïve attitude when it comes to the opposite sex.

Telephone

You need to communicate. If you doodle a mobile phone you want to be contactable anywhere and at any time. Maybe you feel uncomfortable spending time alone or you may need to be constantly surrounded by friends.

To doodle a landline telephone indicates that you are perhaps slightly more grounded but that you still need to communicate. You may be going through a period of loneliness and feel the need to share your woes with someone else.

Also see: Shapes and swirls

Telescope

This reflects a desire to inspect the world around you more closely. You are inquisitive and intelligent, aware of your position in the world and accept that you are only a small part of something bigger. This is a masculine doodle with phallic undertones. You may have somebody in your life to whom you are sexually attracted to, but you are reticent in approaching or revealing your true feelings for them.

Also see: Phallic symbols

Television

This doodle demonstrates a need to know what is going on in the world. It is a thirst for news — both personal and global. The TV is also a cube-like or box-like doodle and therefore you are likely to be practical minded, extremely hard working and meticulous. Your methodical approach also possesses a cautious element. You are likely to enjoy the comforts of home and of a steady domestic life.

Also see: Boxes

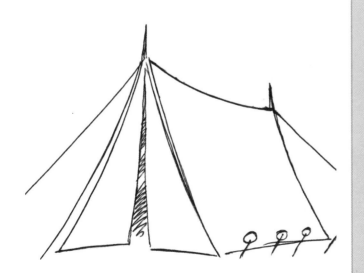

Tent

This doodle shows that you have an interest in outdoor activities and nature. You love to travel and feel as if you have no firm roots in any particular place. You are a nomad at heart.

The entrance to the tent tells us more personal information. A tent with a closed door shows that you are guarded and cautious. You possess a fear of having your personal space invaded. A tent where the door has been left open shows that you are relaxed and social. You love to socialise and entertain and you are extremely warm and hospitable.

Tiger

The tiger doodle shows that you have a very strong sexual appetite, which requires a certain amount of restraint. This is a more feminine doodle than the lion, and may reflect some kind of issue with a maternal figure in your life. You are extremely powerful and ambitious. You also have self-destructive tendencies that need to be kept in check if you are to survive.

Also see: Lion

Tomato — see Food

Tornado

You feel powerless, as though your life were spiralling out of control. You are frustrated and probably extremely angry. You may have obsessive tendencies that are difficult to control and currently you feel overwhelmed and consumed with problems.

Also see: Shapes and swirls

Tortoise

If you doodle a tortoise, you tend to be fairly cautious in your approach to life. You are extremely dependable and methodical in work matters. Sensitive and vulnerable, you may withdraw and become introverted in situations that you find difficult. You have an intense dislike of confrontation. You are imbued with a sense of modesty and reliability.

In Ancient China, the tortoise represented death but in the West the tortoise is a symbol of long life and wisdom.

Also see: Animals

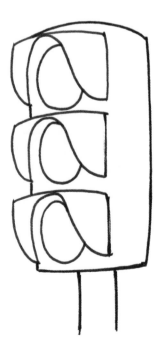

Traffic lights

This is the sign of an extremely busy and active individual. You are creative and possessed with excellent communication skills. You are always to the point and don't suffer fools gladly. If the lights are shaded you may be going through a temporary period of depression. You may seek some kind of change in direction, perhaps professionally.

Also see: Phallic symbols

Train

A train doodle is related to travel and tends to indicate the direction your life is taking. If the train shows carriages, these represent parts of your inner world and your emotional baggage.

A train drawn featuring a driver shows that you feel in control and confident about the direction of your life.

A train drawn on tracks show that you have accepted the direction your life is taking. A train can also represent a need for change and the start of some kind of emotional journey.

Doodles of trains are also phallic and the engine represents the libido. Trains drawn by children tend to mean that they want more independence.

Radio DJ Ken Bruce draws a train, which represents the direction your life is taking

Trees

The tree symbolises the essence of life, and features heavily in religious texts and mythology. Eve picked from the Tree of Knowledge in the Garden of Eden, which led to the loss of innocence and the expulsion of mankind. The Kabala shows a tree of life which represents the universe and human emotions. In mythology, trees bearing fruit are common powerful symbols of life and fertility. There are so many different kinds of trees that it isn't surprising to find people doodle trees in a variety of ways. You'll find this one of the best tests in determining what character traits you display.

A tree drawn with bare branches reveals

British actor Edward Fox of 'Day of the Jackal' fame, doodles a tree

that you are socially uncomfortable and lack patience when dealing with others. You may find it difficult to express your emotions, and as a result you often feel frustrated. You probably find it very difficult to relax and do nothing. Instead, you may throw yourself into your work or career, which is possibly why you are usually successful in this side of your life.

A tree drawn with a big billowy top indicates that you are social, happy and content with your lot in life. You are a very good communicator and very well balanced.

Trees bearing fruit reveal you to be a sensual person with a sociable disposition. You are very

CONTINUED ON PAGE 134

CONTINUED FROM PAGE 133

aware and considerate of others' feelings. You are also deeply romantic.

If you draw Christmas trees, it points towards a strong combative element in you. You are likely to work hard and have a strong ambitious drive. As you find it difficult to obey orders, you can be rather stubborn.

Messy trees show that you are a frustrated person with a creative mind. You have a low opinion of yourself and you need a lot of praise particularly professionally.

Any tree that is drawn with sagging, heavy branches like a weeping willow reveals you to be deeply unhappy. You are very sensitive and retreat into yourself when hurt.

You tend to have a lot of insecurities and you need a vast amount of attention before opening up to others.

A tree that is withered or dead reveals that you are burdened. Perhaps you possess an underlying guilt about an emotional issue. You are likely to suffer from a lack of direction and motivation. You may be finding your life difficult at home, in love and work.

Palm trees show that you love leisure and feel the need to change the direction of your life, so that it is more relaxed and calm. You are enthusiastic and dynamic.

The width and shape of the trunk are important features that also give a lot of clues about who you are. Trees drawn with wide trunks tend to mean you are stable, confident

and well balanced. You prefer long standing monogamous relationships. You also possess a healthy sex drive. Trees with long, thin trunks show you are repressed. You are guided by your head rather than your heart, which in itself may be no bad thing, but it can mean you lack passion.

The backdrop to any doodle of a tree is also an indicator of your state of mind. Trees drawn in fields show you are relaxed and content. You tend to have a stable home life and you are not easily ruffled by anything.

A tree/s drawn on an island reveal you are frightened of solitude. You may find it difficult to make new friends. Your loyalties tend to rest with your family and old friends, and you might be sceptical of new people.

Trees drawn atop of hills show you to be very guarded and emotionally repressed in close relationships. You are essentially a loner who prefers to work in solitude.

Any tree that features shading has a negative connotation. The heaviness and darkness of the shading can reflect the degree of depression you have.

Trees that are drawn chopped down show you are feeling vulnerable and threatened. You may have lost your sense of identity. Perhaps some sort of guilt has caused this.

Trees drawn in clumps reveal you are well balanced and social. You love nature and feel comfortable with the world. You are able to connect easily and closely with others.

Tunnels

This is an overtly sexual doodle that reveals an element of sexual frustration. Perhaps you currently lack motivation — you want to change but you are finding it difficult. You may be feeling quite depressed and trapped. The world has become a very dark place and you would love to find a partner to help you see the light. If you are in a relationship you are probably finding it increasingly claustrophobic and want to escape.

UFOs

These doodles are symbolic of fundamental changes. These changes are usually positive and you are receptive to them. They also show that you are skillfully self-aware. If the illustration features flames or lights you are aware of your wholeness as an individual and consequently very well balanced. You are well equipped to deal with change and new situations in practically any context.

Umbrella

This is a very defensive doodle. The umbrella represents a shield that can be used to guard against things that may hurt you. You may be scared of something and as a consequence you feel anxious. You tend to find it very difficult to relax and you are always protecting yourself from anything you perceive to be threatening, which for you is almost everything.

Unicorn

A doodle of this creature of fantasy reveals you to be an idealist who is a great daydreamer. You are extremely romantic and find it difficult dealing with the practicalities of daily life. There is a purity and innocence in you which gives you childlike qualities. You approach life with the attitude that everything is simple.

A unicorn is also a symbol of change. You have a great sense of aesthetics and you are likely to be a passionate lover.

Also see: Horses

Vampire

The vampire doodle is representative of fear of emotional and sexual relationships. You find these situations threatening and too demanding. You fear losing your independence and you may have had to fight hard to have emancipated yourself from your parents.

You tend to find it difficult to resist temptation which is destructive and harmful. It is difficult to form long lasting relationships as you are possessive and easily become angry with a partner you are in love with. The sharpness of the teeth you draw indicates the severity of your aggression.

Vase

You are essentially relaxed, open, easy-going, friendly and hospitable.

If the vase you draw is empty it shows that you are extremely receptive to change and new ideas.

If the vase has a mass of flowers arranged neatly, you are creative and sensual.

A single stem shows that you have a strong minimalist aesthetic, with a strong drive and clear sense of direction.

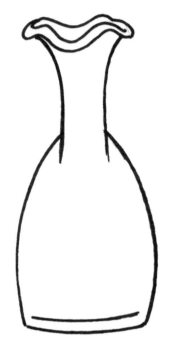

Also see: Flowers

Vegetables — see Food

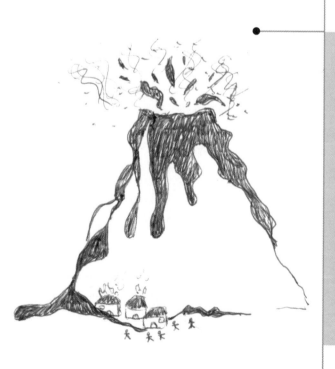

Volcano

A doodle of a volcano represents emotions that have long been suppressed and need to be expressed or shared urgently. If the volcano is erupting these things are about to surface and this can only be positive.

If no eruption is drawn, you may continue to suppress these feelings which will lead to a potentially dangerous situation. You may become increasingly frustrated and bitter and may literally explode with anger if these problems are not addressed and brought out into the open.

Water/waves/reflections

Water is the source of all life and absolutely essential to everything and everyone. To draw water is to reflect your moods and emotions. Water signifies fertility, the maternal influences and destiny. It reveals a search for deeper meaning in life — the deeper the water, the more in-depth this search is. You may also feel that you are being overcome by emotions and literally drowning in them. Calm, deep water shows a sense of serenity and peace within you. You are contemplative, and have a relaxed sense of humour. If the water appears choppy, you may be suffering some

turbulent emotional times, and feel threatened and confused. Messy, chaotic waves reflect an inability to make an important decision because you feel too emotional. If the water appears to be hot (i.e. maybe you've drawn a hot natural spring, with steam ensuing) then you have fear of being hurt and you may be facing some social problems. There is an underlying fluid sexuality in all doodles featuring water. Reflections that may be depicted are also very revealing. Contemplation of the self and anxiety about your appearance may be some trait particular to you. If figures are represented in a mirror or on the surface of the water, they generally represent you, and denote an obsession with self-image.

Weapons

These are masculine phallic symbols. As there is so much weapon imagery both in movies, animation and cartoons, it's unsuprising that there are weapon doodles. If you draw axes, guns and knives dripping with blood, while they can mean nothing more than the memory of a movie you have just watched or a cartoon you have just read, if doodled frequently it can reveal that you are troubled, aggressive, and sexually frustrated. Obsessive doodling of these and nothing else may have more sinister implications. You may display a strong sadistic streak — in the form of self-destruction or aggression towards others. This anger could be rooted in your relationship with a maternal or

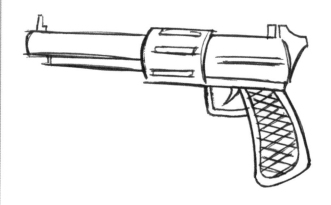

paternal figure. If, however, you just doodle these from time to time it shows you are temporarily angry but not pathologically so. Your anger is probably caused by some kind of flash in the pan argument and will be short lived. If you are a female doodler and you draw guns, it shows frustration and hostility towards a male partner or men in general. If you are male, you may feel sexually frustrated and you are attempting to reassert your masculinity. Drawing overtly masculine doodles is an attempt to cover up your softer side. Knives and swords are hugely phallic. They can also indicate sexual repression, as well as a desire to injure somebody emotionally. You feel frustrated and perhaps you find it difficult to express your anger.

Webs

A web drawn on its own reveals that you feel trapped and unhappy in your life. You feel lost and powerless and you are becoming increasingly frustrated. These sentiments may stem from a difficult work situation or partnership issues. You are clever, and at times you can be manipulative. A web can have a similar appearance to a maze or a labyrinthine doodle. Sometimes a web can be interpreted as a desire for protection — you literally want to cocoon yourself or hide away. Overall it represents a need for change.

Also see: Maze

Wheel

Drawing wheels shows that you are receptive to change, and that you are aware of the ups and downs in life. You may be feeling that you are not in control of your life. This is specifically evidenced by drawing a steering wheel. Perhaps you are under too much pressure to express the real you. The wheel shows that there are some changes to be made in your life or your approach to life, but only you know how to do this.

Also see: Circles

Window

A window reveals you are a social, outward-looking individual. Drawn with people inside, a window shows you to be welcoming and hospitable. You enjoy a stable family life and have good, solid relationships. Lots of windows mean you are inquisitive, even bordering on nosy. If you doodle someone climbing out of a window, you may be avoiding confrontation. Someone climbing into a window shows you could be withdrawing into yourself or you are desperately trying to understand someone else. The height/length of the window shows how comfortable you are with what you see in your life. The smaller the window the more anxious and afraid you are of the world outside.

Witch

A witch represents the fears and complex feelings you have in relationships. These have been turned into repeated patterns that have been established within maternal relationships. For the female doodler, an element of self-loathing may be apparent depending on the degree of ugliness featured. A monstrous witch could imply that you feel guilty for being cruel in a loving relationship, or it may represent somebody else who you feel threatened by or fear. If the witch is attractive, it implies that you are wise, harmless and have a huge capacity and desire for spirituality. You are at ease with yourself. If you are a male doodler of witches, the witch may represent a woman you dislike or feel intimidated by.

Wizards

You may be interested in the occult and believe in magic. You are very dreamy and have an obsessive thirst for knowledge. A good sense of humour is apparent.

Once again the face may denote what you think of yourself. A long beard would suggest that you feel content, relaxed and confident in your judgement. You are as wise as the wizard, or at least you would like everyone to think so. If the wizard's face is shown as a particularly old man, it could represent an anxiety of growing old.

Also see: Faces and Hair

Wolf

You may be feeling hunted or persecuted, but the strongest element represented here is fear. If you are a female doodler, it represents an anxiety about men and of your sexuality. As a male doodler, it implies you are sexually frustrated which could mean you adopt a rather predatory style in attempting to attract a mate. A wolf that is drawn with very sharp teeth shows you have an aggressive side that appears when you feel threatened. You are likely to have a strong survival instinct.

Yacht — see Boat